ALFRED THE GREAT

ALFRED THE GREAT.
Statue by Hamo Thornycroft, ·R.A.

Alfred the Great

CONTAINING

Chapters on his Life and Times

BY

MR. FREDERIC HARRISON, THE LORD BISHOP OF BRISTOL
PROFESSOR CHARLES OMAN, SIR CLEMENTS MARKHAM
THE REV. PROFESSOR EARLE, SIR FREDERICK POLLOCK
AND THE REV. W. J. LOFTIE; ALSO CONTAINING
AN INTRODUCTION BY SIR WALTER BESANT
AND A POEM BY THE POET LAUREATE

EDITED, WITH PREFACE, BY

ALFRED BOWKER

*'This will I say—that I have sought to live worthily the while I lived,
and after my life to leave to the men that come after me
a remembering of me in good works.'*

BOOKS FOR LIBRARIES PRESS
FREEPORT, NEW YORK

First Published 1899
Reprinted 1971

INTERNATIONAL STANDARD BOOK NUMBER:
0-8369-5760-1

LIBRARY OF CONGRESS CATALOG CARD NUMBER:
78-154144

PRINTED IN THE UNITED STATES OF AMERICA

TO

Her Majesty the Queen

BY GRACIOUS PERMISSION

THIS VOLUME

IS

DEDICATED

THE SPOTLESS KING

I

Some lights there be within the Heavenly Spheres
Yet unrevealed, the interspace so vast :
So through the distance of a thousand years
Alfred's full radiance shines on us at last.

II

Star of the spotless fame, from far-off skies
Teaching this truth, too long not understood,
That only they are worthy who are wise,
And none are truly great that are not good.

III

Of valour, virtue, letters, learning, law,
Pattern and prince, His name will now abide,
Long as of conscience Rulers live in awe,
And love of country is their only pride.

IV

But with His name four other names attune,
Which from oblivion guardian Song may save ;
Lone Athelney, victorious Ethandune,
Wantage his cradle, Winchester his grave.

ALFRED AUSTIN.

PREFACE

Now that we are fast approaching the one thousandth anniversary of the death of our greatest sovereign of the past—"King Alfred," whom it is the laudable desire of many of Her Majesty's subjects and others to commemorate fittingly—this book, which bears the king's name, and is written in honour of the king, and is intended to present what is known of the king's achievements and his claim on the gratitude and love of the English-speaking race, would hardly seem to demand a preface.

To some minds, however, this small book, if it appeared without a word of preface, might seem insufficiently comprehensive ; it may be well, therefore, to explain shortly the motive for its production. The International Committee organising this Commemoration have considered it very advisable that a publication should be issued with a view to diffusing, as widely as possible, public knowledge of the king's life and work. This being the sole object, it became essential that the book should not be costly, but within the reach of all.   Therefore it was also necessary to restrict its scope ; numerous subjects and possible illustrations of interest have been left for a full and complete biography of the great king.

At the same time, it is hoped that the chapters which follow will enable the general reader to create in his own mind a figure, a mind, a history, worthy of the king and equal to the occasion. The general introduction is, in substance, the address delivered in the Guildhall of Winchester by Sir Walter Besant at the first public meeting held to lay the foundation stone of this Commemoration.   The names of those who have contributed chapters are a guarantee that the reader is in good hands ; the subjects of these chapters show a fairly complete division of the various lines in which Alfred achieved greatness.

Whilst taking this opportunity of placing on record my very cordial thanks to the contributors for their gifts, especially to Sir Walter Besant, and to the Lord Bishop of Winchester for kindly advice, I feel that my thanks alone would indeed be a poor requite ; but our readers, of whatever station, whether high or low, by assisting to the best of their ability in the forthcoming Commemoration, which is veritably that of one thousand years of many of our institutions, of our government, and our national existence, will be expressing gratitude and thanks more acceptable than words of mine can convey.

It may seem strange to some readers that by chance no full account is given of Asser's anecdote of the scene between the king and the herdswoman in the Isle of Athelney, where he took refuge, but as the story is known to all, its omission may perhaps be pardoned ; it is certainly not due to any lack of interest in the story, which seems so strikingly to show that at times, maybe when the king was resting or sitting by the fire mending his bows and weapons, he would become absorbed in the one thought foremost in his mind—that of the welfare of his country and people, then sorely harassed and oppressed by the Danes, and so neglected the homely duty that was present.

I have, further, to draw the reader's attention to the circular at the end of the book, but it is not necessary for me to point out the advisability, or to detail the many praiseworthy reasons, for the erection of memorials to illustrious dead, stimulating and encouraging as they are to succeeding generations, engendering patriotic sentiments, and recalling to us the history of the past by which knowledge is weighed and gained, and that from the lesson we learn almost unwittingly to shape and guide our future steps.

In conclusion, I would express a hope that the following chapters will be read far and wide with as much pleasure and profit as they have been by myself, and that through their agency, and out of public subscription, we may soon see rising in the heart of the capital of Wessex, worthy not of England alone, but of the English-speaking race, a memorial to one who may rightly be regarded as one of the principal founders of the English nation and its language, a pioneer of improvement, liberty, learning and education, and who, though a thousand years have sped, still forms a mighty beacon of all the highest aims and the noblest aspirations that may dominate the hearts of men.

A. B.

1st May 1899.

CONTENTS

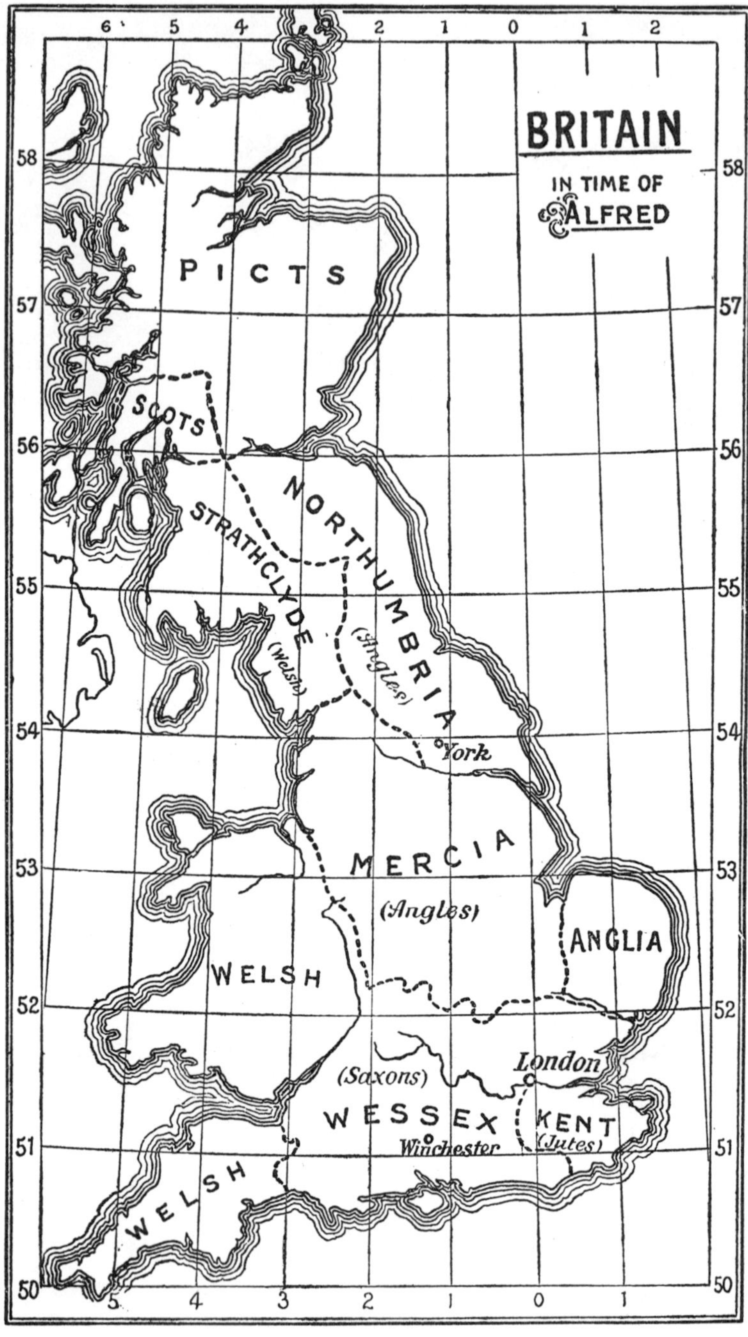

BRITAIN
IN TIME OF
ALFRED
PICTS
SCOTS
STRATHCLYDE
(Welsh)
NORTHUMBRIA
(Angles)
York
MERCIA
(Angles)
ANGLIA
WELSH
(Saxons)
London
WESSEX
KENT
(Jutes)
Winchester
WELSH

INTRODUCTION

N writing an Introduction to the chapters which follow, I shall not be expected to contribute any new facts to the life of the great king. As for any new facts, the time has long gone by when anything new could be discovered concerning the great king of whom I have to speak. The tale of Alfred is a twice-told tale : but it is a tale that should be always fresh and new, because at every point it concerns every successive generation of English-speaking people. Happily it is not the whole life of Alfred that we have to consider in this place : it is the example of that life : the things that Alfred invented and achieved during that short life for his own generation ; things which have lasted to our own day, and still bear fruit and golden sheaves. I should like to proceed at once to those achievements, but it is absolutely necessary first that we should understand some of the conditions of the time : the troubles and the struggles : the overthrow and ruin with which Alfred's reign began :

the apparent hopelessness of the situation changed by the unexpected uprising of one man : and the rapid development of this man as Captain, Conqueror, Administrator, and Teacher. This done, we shall be in a position to receive the King as an example that should abide with the people still, and should still continue to shape the lives and inspire the minds of his race.

In order to prevent long explanations, and to illustrate at the outset some of the conditions of England when Alfred was born into the world, I have caused a small map to be drawn. You will see that the island is divided up into many nations. There is first the Kingdom of Kent, founded by the Jutes, who never extended themselves : then the Kingdom of Wessex or of the West Saxons, who by this time had absorbed the Kingdom of Essex or East Saxons, and of Sussex or South Saxons. The modern counties of Norfolk and Suffolk form the Kingdom of East Anglia— founded by Angles, a people closely allied to Jutes and Saxons : the middle of England is Mercia, the Kingdom of the March or boundary—the Mercians were also Angles. On the north is the Kingdom of Northumbria, also founded by Angles. The West of England is wholly occupied by Strathclyde, Wales, and Cornwall, all kingdoms of the Britons or Welsh who remained still unconquered. In Scotland the Highlands were occupied by the

Picts, and a part of the west was peopled by the Scots who crossed over from Ireland. The Angles therefore occupied the middle, the north, and the east ; they gave their own name to the whole country — Angle-land or England : the Saxons occupied the south, with the exception of Kent : the Welsh still held nearly the whole of the west : but their territories were separated and cut into three parts. If we look backwards and forwards in history during these centuries we shall find the map of our island constantly changing. But still we may take this map fairly to represent the country as it was in the time of Alfred — eight distinct nations in it : three of them composed of Angles, who were not on that account allies : one containing Jutes : one of Saxons : three of Welsh. These so-called nations shifted their borders continually : they fought their neighbours : they split up and fought each other : there was no coherence or stability among them : some of them adopted Christianity and then relapsed : some of them remained pagans.

These were the tribes or nations in the land.

Let us next consider what manner of men it was over whom Alfred was called upon to rule. In order to get at this knowledge we must inquire of their religion, their laws, and their customs. As for their religion, before they became Christians, it was a fierce and cruel religion, although it was full of imagination, as was to be expected of a people in whose minds the noblest poetry was slumbering. There were Gods who created and invented : Gods who gave life and inspired love : Gods who sent the thunder and the storm : Gods who brought the spring and the sunshine, the fruit, and the harvest. There were evil Gods—the Gods of Death, who killed men : the Gods of Disease, who tortured men : the Gods of the Sea and the River, who drowned men : the Gods of Battle, who struck men with cowardice, and weighed down their hands so that they could not strike. There were humbler deities—spirits of the stream, the woods, and the hills—for the most part hostile to men and malignant, because in certain stages of civilisation the unknown forces of Nature present themselves as personal deities who are always hostile to man —according to the Greek legend, for instance, he who met the great God Pan face to face fell down dead. They believed in raising spirits and in spectres, much as some of us do now : they believed in witches and in witchcraft : in magic and in charms : in love philtres : in divination : in lucky days. In a word, the Anglo-Saxon was full of the superstitions which belonged to his age.

There was, however—I venture to read between the lines—one saving clause. The Anglo-Saxon was not only afraid of the unknown, which caused him to invent malignant deities, but in his mind the God of Creation was stronger than the God of Destruction. There is hope for a people while that belief survives. Long after he became a Christian the Saxon continued to retain his old beliefs under other names: he saw and conversed in imagination with the old deities whom he had forsaken: they spoke to him in the thunder: he saw their forms in the flying cloud, in the splendour of the sunset: he heard their whispers in the woods: they came to him in dreams. Religion, to the Anglo-Saxon, was a thing more real, more present, than it has ever been to any people except the Russian and the Jew. This is perhaps the most important point to be observed in the character of Alfred's people. They were profoundly influenced by their religion. In the eighth century, when Christianity was spread over the south and the middle of the country, all classes began to long after the religious life as they understood it. Kings and Queens—there were ten Kings and eleven Queens—Princes and Princesses, nobles and freemen—all who could be received, crowded into the monasteries: they were eager for the life of meditation and of prayer: they made the cloisters rich: they filled the monastic houses with gold and silver plate and rich treasure. When the Danish invasion began, the Danes very soon found out that it was the monastery, and not the town, which they should sack: and at the same

time the people found out that the full monastery
meant the shrunken army.   It has been said that
the Anglo-Saxon never changes.   In this respect
at least he has never changed.   Through all the
changes and chances of a thousand years, wherever
he has penetrated, wherever he has settled, he has
carried with him the same earnestness and the same
reality of religion.

We must also note, next to the earnestness of
his religious belief, the freedom of his institutions.
The liberties of our race, which have become to
us like the very air we breathe, so that we are not
even conscious of them, were not wrested by the
people from reluctant kings.   These liberties had
always been with them from the prehistoric times
when the family was the unit, and when custom
was the only kind of law.   Among their primitive
customs were the first rude forms of their free
institutions.   From the Forests of North Germany,
from the mouth of the Elbe, not from any king,
came the right of free meeting : the right of free
speech : the right of free thought : the right of
free work.

Next, as a people the Saxons were also fond of
music, singing, poetry : the quicker witted Norman
despised the Saxon as slow of understanding.
Perhaps : but the Saxon proved himself in the
long-run far more capable of enthusiasm, of
loyalty, of patriotism, of sacrifice, of all those

actions and emotions which spring from the imagination and produce forces united and irresistible. Remember that the whole of our literature is Anglo-Saxon ; none of it is Norman. There is not one great Norman poet. No Norman literature was produced on this our Anglo-Saxon soil.

The next characteristic of this people is less picturesque. They were obstinate. Now obstinacy, if we think of it, is one of the most useful and valuable qualities that can be planted in the breast of man. It has many names : it is called by its friends firmness : under any name it is the tenacious man who wins in the long-run.

They were essentially an outdoor people : they loved all manner of outdoor sports : all classes were hunters, hawkers, fishers, trappers : the country was full of creatures to hunt : there were in the forests wolves, bears, wild bulls, and stags : they loved the free air of the open hillside : and they hated towns. It was many years after their settlement in this country before they ceased to feel the old terror of the magic which, they thought, could be practised within the walls of a city.

As regards the Anglo-Saxon women, it is pleasant to learn that the very same virtues which are now conspicuous in our own women of the present day were conspicuous in them. She was, as Thomas Wright says, " An attentive housewife : a tender companion : the comforter and consoler of her husband and her family : the virtuous and noble matron." In all ranks, from the queen to the farmer's wife, we find the lady of the household attending to her household duties. They were more learned than the men : they could recite and sing the poetry of their native bards : they were skilful in playing the harp : and in embroidery and needlework of all kinds the work of the Anglo-Saxon ladies was in demand all over Western Europe.

The Anglo-Saxon, therefore, had many virtues. He had also, we must confess, his faults, which were conspicuous as well as numerous. He was slothful of mind : he was always ready to sink back to the ancient seclusion of the village and the forest : he was conservative, and thought the old ways would last for ever : he was a great drinker—in drinking, except among the Danes, he had no equal : he would drink for days together almost without stopping : even the priests did not escape the universal vice : they were admonished by the bishops not to say mass unless they were sober : his hospitality consisted chiefly in making the guests drunk. The Saxons, again, have been charged with cruelty—certainly very terrible things were done, but we cannot expect a people to be before their age : it was a cruel age. Frenchman, Norman, Dane, Saxon : all alike were cruel in their punishments : but these things belong to the time. Let us acquit the people of Wessex of more than their share of the average cruelty. The stories told of the Danes, for example, are almost incredible, whether for the cruelty of the torture, or for the endurance of the victim.

When we say that the Anglo-Saxon was a free man, and governed by free laws, we must not imagine him to be a Republican of the nineteenth century. Nor must we conclude that the Anglo-Saxon was a democrat, as we understand democracy. He had his king over him, to begin with : and the king was not elected by the people from among themselves, as the President of a Republic ; he succeeded because he belonged to the Royal blood. He was even allowed, long after they were Christians, to be descended from the Gods : the people consented to his succession, but they did not elect him. As king he had very large powers, and these were undefined : men had not yet begun to question the Royal Prerogative : above all, he was their captain : he led the army : he fought with the army.

In a word, the Anglo-Saxon of the ninth century was in essentials very much like his descendant of the present day. He was religious : he was a lover of order: he was a good fighting man: he was fond of outdoor sports and occupations : he was tenacious of his freedom : he was imaginative, poetical, and dreamy : he was fond of music : he was still full of the old traditions and superstitions which ruled his life, long after he had become a Christian. This is a general summary of his character. In one virtue he was as yet wanting. We must not expect in him what we call the national and patriotic sentiment. The man of Wessex was the enemy of the man of Mercia : the north stood aloof. from the south : there was no England or Britain : there was only a large island divided among eight nations, or ten nations, or five nations, according to the year of the Lord : some of them spoke the same tongue : all the Angles, Jutes, and Saxons had similar institutions : nevertheless they were enemies. You remember, two hundred years later on, how London accepted the rule, first, of Cnut the Dane : and, next, of William the Norman. Both of them were what we should call foreigners. There was no such feeling then. To the Londoner it mattered little whether his king was Mercian, Northumbrian, Saxon, Jute, Dane, or Norman. London received kings from all these people. There was not yet any feeling existing for the country as a whole. It was part of the work of Alfred, unseen and un-suspected, to make it possible to weld the different nations into one : to create little by little the love of country in place of the old loyalty to the tribe.

Let us concede that Alfred fought, not for England, but for Wessex. In doing so, it is true, he fought for all England, but perhaps without his knowledge. In the same way David fought first for his own little country—for Judea—and made it possible for his successor to create one great country, of which Judea was the centre.

I have lingered a long time over the character of the people whom Alfred was called upon to rule. Without this knowledge it is impossible to understand what the king did and why he did it, and in what respects his work is so truly remarkable and wonderful. Let us now pass on to the history itself, and first, naturally, to the invasions of the Danes.

It was in the year 832—seventeen years before the birth of Alfred—that the Danes first made their appearance on these shores. Their incursions began and continued exactly in the same way as those of the Saxons themselves 400 years before. They came over in their ships : they found the north seas without defence : they found no fleets guarding the island from the pirates, as of old : the people, ready to believe that things would go on for ever unaltered, had actually abandoned their ships ; had lost the art of ship-building ; and were no longer accustomed to the sea. The Danish fleet swooped down upon the coast: harried the country : murdered the people : sacked the monasteries and the churches, and went away again. They found the coast, like the seas, defenceless : the monastic houses had drained the country of the fighting nobles : the warlike spirit of the people was wasting itself in petty tribal wars. The Danes, until the old spirit returned, were far more than a match for the Saxons. They appeared suddenly, without warning, now on the coast of Kent : now on that of Dorsetshire : now at the mouth of the Parret, in Somerset : now up the Thames : now at Southampton : they came in fleets of a hundred and fifty ships, carrying each sixty or seventy warriors : an army greater than anything that could be hastily got together against them : by the time that an army was collected the Danes had gone, leaving ruined churches : villages destroyed by fire : monasteries pillaged of their treasures : and murdered monks lying beside the scattered relics, which could not protect them. The Danes, their foray over, had gone off, bearing their treasures with them, to their own country. Next year they landed again : but on another part of the island.

This yearly invasion of the Danes lasted for twenty years. They always made straight for the nearest monasteries, which they sacked : there were not many towns in Saxon England ; but there were some — Canterbury, London, Southampton, York—they attacked these, seized, plundered, and left them in ruins. For twenty years they came every year : sometimes we hear of a victory over them : but still they came again : there was never a victory so decisive as to keep them from returning in ever-increasing numbers. Then they began to stay in the country : they left off going home in the autumn : they established themselves in winter quarters, first on Sheppey Island, then on the Isle of Thanet : then in Norfolk. Then they went farther afield. In a word, they overran and conquered East Anglia : then the Kingdom of Northumbria : then that of Mercia : then the united Kingdoms of Wessex and Kent. It was at this crisis, when all the power of the Danes was brought to bear against Wessex and Kent, Alfred succeeded to the throne. His father and his four brothers, kings one after the other, had spent their lives in vainly beating back hordes of the Danes, who returned year after year. The Anglo-Saxon Chronicle makes the best of occasional victories, but the fact remains that every year the invaders became stronger and the defenders became weaker. The King of Mercia at last gave up the struggle and went to Rome, to adopt the religious life, leaving his wife behind. Alfred might have done the same thing, and it would not have been imputed unto him for cowardice, but for godliness.

Happily for England he did not. The Danes

had seized Chippenham, in Wiltshire, and made that place their stronghold and headquarters. From Chippenham they sent out their light troops, moving rapidly here and there, devastating and murdering. For nine long years, growing every year weaker, Alfred fought them : in one year he fought nine battles. At the end of that time he found himself deserted, save for a few faithful followers : his country prostrate : everything in the hands of the enemy : his cause lost, and apparently no loop-hole or glimmer of hope left of recovery. No darker or more gloomy time ever fell upon this country. Everywhere the churches and the monasteries were pillaged and destroyed. All those—bishops, priests, monks, and nuns—who could get away had fled, carrying with them such of their treasures as they could convey. The towns were in ruins : the farms were deserted : the people had lost hope and heart : they bowed their heads and entered into slavery : their religion was destroyed with the flight or the murder of their priests. Their arts, their learning, their civilisation, all that they had once possessed, were destroyed in those nine years' warfare : destroyed and gone—it seemed for ever. And the king, with his wife and her sister, and his children, and the few who still remained with him, had taken refuge on a little hill rising out of a broad marsh, whither the enemy could not follow him.

In the after years Alfred was fond of talking over this time of desolation : he would recall the visions that came to him, and not only to him but to his wife as well : they both saw visions of consolation and of promise. Saint Cuthbert himself stood beside his bed and comforted him with promise of victory and honour. We can very well believe the vision. To Alfred : to his wife : the aid of the Saints was a thing to be invoked and to be looked for. Did they not pray daily for the help of the Saints? And who should aid the Saxons in their trouble but their greatest Saint— Cuthbert himself? In the sleep or the waking of night, what more natural than that Alfred should imagine that he saw and spoke with the Saint himself? To those who drive or walk across the dreary level of Sedgemoor, now drained by its deep dykes, and dotted with its village churches, there rises on the right hand the low hill of Athelney. One can realise, looking upon this hill across the flat land, which was once covered with bogs and quagmires, and reeds bending before the wind, how complete was the defeat of the king : how complete the victory of the Danes ; which should drive Alfred to seek such a refuge. The Danish Conquest, like the Norman Conquest two hundred years later, seemed an achievement accomplished. No further opposition : no one asked what had become of Alfred—he had run away to Rome :

he had gone into a monastery, perhaps : everywhere the Danes all over the country reported submission and the acceptance of their rule. And the old gods had come back again, Woden, and Thor, and Friga, and the rest : and again the fires flamed upon the high places, and the children were passed through them, and all the Christian saints had fled.

Alfred remained inactive during the whole long winter. It was the rule of the old Kriegs Spiel, the war game of that time, that the armies should not go forth to fight in winter. The men would have refused to go out in the cold season. In fact, they could not. The country was covered with uncleared forests : the roads in winter were deep tracks of mud : it was impossible for the men to sleep on the cold, wet ground. The delay suited Alfred : he wanted time to organise a rising in force : he sent messengers to the Somersetshire people, among whom, in winter quarters, were lying few or none of the Danish conquerors : he bade them make ready for the spring : he ordered those of the thanes who were still left to come to him at Athelney : and in May, when the spring arrived, Alfred appeared once more as one risen from the dead : once more he raised the Wessex standard of the Golden Dragon : once more the people, taking renewed courage, flocked together : as he marched along they joined him, the fugitives from the woods and those who had been made slaves in their own farms, and swelled his force.

What follows is like a dream. Or it is like the uprising of the French under Joan of Arc. There had been nine years of continuous defeat. The people had lost heart : they had apparently given in. Yet, on the reappearance of their king, they sprang to arms once more : they followed him with one consent, and on the first encounter with the Danes they inflicted upon them a defeat so crushing that they never rallied again. In one battle, on one field, the country was recovered. In a single fortnight after this battle the Danes were turned out of Wessex. Alfred had recovered the whole of his own country, and acquired in addition a large part of Mercia.

It is significant to read that the Danish chieftain became a Christian, and was baptized. Do you suppose that he weighed the arguments and listened to the history and the doctrines of the new religion ? Not at all. He perceived—this logical pagan—that King Alfred's Gods had shown their superiority over his own in a manner so unexpected, so amazing, and so decisive, that he hesitated no longer. He acknowledged that superiority ; he was baptized, and he never afterwards relapsed.

Alfred had got back his kingdom. It remained

for him to recover it in a fuller and a larger sense :
to restore its former prosperity and its ancient
strength.

He began by recognising the separate rights of
the Mercians. He would not call himself King of
Mercia. He placed his son-in-law Ethelred as
Earl of Mercia, and because London was at that
time considered a Mercian city, Ethelred took up
his residence there as soon as the Danes had
gone out. The condition of London was as desolate and as ruinous as that of the whole country.
The walls were falling down : there was no trade :
there were no ships in the river : no merchandise
on the wharves : there were no people in the
streets, save the Danish soldiers and the slaves
who worked for them. Alfred restored the
walls : rebuilt the gates : brought back trade and
merchants : repaired the Bridge, and made London
once more the most important city of his kingdom : its strongest defence : its most valuable
possession. This was, in fact, the third foundation of London. If Alfred had failed to understand the importance of London — that great
port, happily placed, not on the coast open to
attack, but a long way up a tidal river, in the very
heart of the country—a place easy of access from
every part of the kingdom—a port convenient for
every kind of trade, whether from the Baltic or
the Mediterranean—the whole of the commercial

history of England would have been changed, the island might have remained what it had been for centuries before the Roman Conquest, a place which exported iron, tin, skins, wool, and slaves, and imported for the most part weapons to kill each other with.

Alfred gave us London. The lesson of ten years' fighting taught Alfred what the Saxons had never before understood, the value of walled cities in the case of invasion. He saw — he was the first to perceive—how superior numbers may be rendered of no avail when they fling themselves against strong walls. The next Danish invaders found themselves stopped on their way up the Thames by a city fortified by a strong wall which the enemy could neither knock down nor climb over : and manned by citizens made doubly courageous by the safety and the strength of their ramparts. Six separate sieges were endured by London during the second invasion of the Danes : six separate times the enemy had to raise the siege and to go elsewhere, leaving London unconquered. Other walled towns were added — Winchester, York, Exeter, and Canterbury—but the first was London, whose fallen Roman wall, of which only the hard core of cement remained, Alfred rebuilt and faced again with stone.

Alfred, I repeat, gave us London. This was a great service which he rendered to the safety of the country.   But there was still a greater service. The Saxon had quite forgotten the seamanship in which he had formerly known no master and no equal.   Alfred saw that for the sake of safety there must be a first line of defence before the coast could be reached.   England could only be invaded in ships, and by those who had the command of the seas.   Therefore, he created a navy : he built ships longer, heavier, swifter than those of the Danes, and he sent these ships out to meet the Danes on what they supposed to be their own element.   They went out : they met the Danes : they defeated them : and before long the Saxons had afloat a fleet of a hundred ships to hold the mastery of the Channel.   The history of the English navy is chequered : there have been periods when its pretensions were low and its achievements humble : but since the days of Alfred the conviction has never been lost that the safety of England lies in her command of the sea.   Fortresses and walled cities are useful : it is a very great achievement to have given them to the country : London alone, restored by Alfred, was the nation's stronghold, the nation's treasure house, a city full of wealth, filled with valiant citizens, unconquered and defiant : that was a very great gift to the country : but it was a greater achievement still to have given to the country a fleet which was ready to meet the enemy before they had time to land, and to give them most excellent reasons why they should not land : to make the people understand that above all things, and before all, it was necessary for all time to keep the mastery of the seas.

Remember, therefore, that Alfred, thus, gave us the command of the seas.

As Rudyard Kipling, our patriot poet, says :

> We have fed our seas for a thousand years,
>   And she calls us, still unfed,
> Though there's never a wave of all her waves
>   But marks our English dead.

"Never a wave of all her waves"—and it was Alfred who first sent out the English blood to redden those waves in defence of hearth and home.

Now, there can be no doubt that if he had advanced upon the great defeat of the Danes he might have recovered the whole of the country and become not only its overlord, as his grand-father Egbert had been before him, but its king. No doubt he was tempted : to a successful commander more successes always lie before him waiting to be snatched. This dream of conquest he renounced. He sat down with what he had— the old kingdom of his forefathers, strengthened by his new fleet : by the stronghold of London : and by the restored courage and self-respect of his people. The dream of conquest was a dream of personal ambition : he put it aside. It was part of that renunciation of self which belongs to the whole of his career. The historian Green has pointed out that Alfred "is the only instance in the history of Christendom of a ruler who put aside every personal aim or ambition in order to devote himself wholly to the welfare of those whom he ruled."

We have considered Alfred as a captain, a conqueror, and the founder of our navy. We will now consider him in the capacity of king, administrator, and law-giver.

I do not claim for Alfred that he was the creator of the English law. His glory consists mainly in his adaptation of the old order to the new : he took all that was left of the shattered past and moulded it anew, with additions to suit the new situation, and for the most part on the same lines. You will ask, perhaps, how much of the honour due to Alfred's achievements should be given to his ministers and how much to himself? Assign to his officers all the credit possible, all that belongs to the faithful discharge of duty : still the initiative, the design of the whole of the past, is absolutely due to Alfred himself. He must not be considered as a modern king—the modern king reigns while the people rule : he was the king who ruled : his will ruled the land : he had his Parliament : his Meeting of the Wise : but his will ruled them : he appointed his earls or aldermen : his will ruled them : he had his bishops : his will ruled them. From the time when he began to address himself to the organisation of a strong nation— that is to say, from the time when the Dane was baptized, his will ruled supreme. No law existed then to limit the king's prerogative. The king was imperator, commander of the army, and every man in the country was his soldier.

Among the monuments of his reign there stands out pre-eminent his code of laws. He did not, I say, originate or invent his code. He simply took the old code and rewrote it, with additions and alterations to suit the altered conditions of the time. He understood, in fact, the great truth, which law-makers hardly ever grasp, that successful institutions must be *the outcome of national character*. Now, the laws and customs of these nations —Saxons, Angles, and Jutes—were similar, but there were differences. They had grown with the people, and were the outcome of the national character. Alfred took over as the foundation of his work for Wessex the code compiled for the West Saxons by his ancestor, King Ina : for Mercia, that compiled by Offa, King of Mercia : for the Jutes, that compiled by Ethelbert, King of Kent. In his work two main principles guided the law-giver : first, that justice should be provided for every one, high and low, rich and poor : next, that the Christian religion should be recognised as containing the Law of God : which must be the basis of all laws. Both these principles were especially necessary to be observed at this time. The devastation of the long wars had caused justice to be neglected : and the destruction of the churches, and the murder or flight of the clergy, had caused the people to relapse into their old superstitions.

King Alfred then boldly began his code by reciting the Laws of God. His opening words were: "Thus saith the Lord, 'I am the Lord thy God.'" That is his keynote. The laws of a people must conform with the Laws of God. If they are contrary to the spirit of these laws they cannot be righteous laws. In order that every one might himself compare his laws with the Laws of God, he prefaced his laws first by the Ten Commandments ; after this he quoted at length certain chapters of the Mosaic Law. These chapters he followed by the short epistle in the Acts of the Apostles concerning what should be expected and demanded of Christians. Finally, Alfred adds the precept from St. Matthew, "Whatsoever ye would that men should do to you, do ye even so to them."

Some writers have assumed that Alfred required of his subjects by this preamble that they should be governed in all the details of life by the Mosaic Law. This view I cannot accept. Alfred set forth, I think, these laws in order that his own might

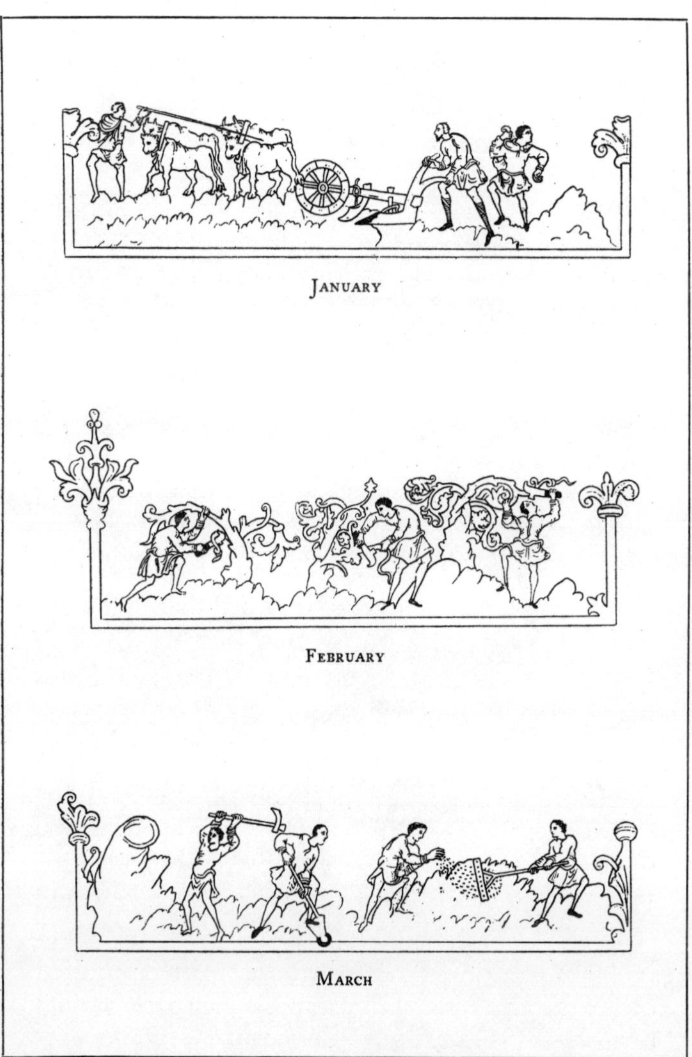

THE SEASONS—JANUARY TO MARCH

be compared with them where comparison was possible, and in order to challenge comparison and to give the greater weight to his own laws by showing that they were based in spirit and, *mutatis mutandis*, on the Levitical Law and on the Law of the Gospel.

Moreover, in order to connect the whole system of justice with religion, in order to teach the people in the most efficacious manner possible that the Church desires justice above all things, he added to the sentence of the judge the penance of the Church. This subjection of the law to the Church would seem intolerable to us. At that time it was necessary to make a rude, ignorant, and violent people understand that religion must be more than a creed : that it must have a practical and restraining side ; a man who was made to understand that an offence against the law was an offence against the Church which would be punished by the latter as well as by the secular judge, was made for the first time to feel the reality of the Church.

This firm determination to link the Divine Law and the Human Law : this firm reliance on the Divine Law as the foundation of all law : is to me the most characteristic point in the whole of Alfred's work. The view—the intention—the purpose of King Alfred are summed up, without intention, by the poet whom I have already quoted. The following words of Rudyard Kipling might be the very words of Alfred : they breathe his very spirit—they might be, I say, the very words spoken by Alfred :

Keep ye the law : be swift in all obedience—
Clear the land of evil : drive the road and bridge the ford.
    Make ye sure to each his own
    That he reap where he hath sown :
By the Peace among our Peoples let men know we serve
    the Lord !

Alfred endeavoured to rebuild the monasteries. He then made the discovery that the old passion for the monastic life was gone : he could get no one to go into them. Forty years of a life and death struggle had killed the desire for the cloister : the people had learned to love action better than seclusion—their ideal was now the soldier, not the monk. A great gain for the people, which never afterwards returned to its ancient love of the Rule and the Hood.

His chief design in rebuilding the monasteries was to restore the schools. The country had fallen so low in learning that there was hardly a single priest who could translate the Church Service into Saxon, or could understand the words he sang. Alfred sent abroad for scholars : he made his Religious House not only a place for the retreat of pious men and women, but also the home—the only possible home—of learning, and the seat of schools. It is long since we have regarded a monastery as a seat of learning, or the proper place for a school. Go back to Alfred's time and consider what a monastery meant in a land still full of violence : in which morals had been lost: justice trampled down: learning destroyed: no schools or teachers left : the monastery stood as an example and a reminder of self-restraint : peace : and order : a life of industry and such works as the most ignorant must acknowledge to be good: where the poor and the sick were received and cared for : the young were taught : and the old sheltered. It was the Life which the monastery Rule profeſſed ; the aim rather than any lower standards accepted by the monks : which made a monastery in that age like a beacon steadily and brightly burning, so that the people had always before their eyes a reminder of the self-governed life. Most of us would be very unwilling to see the monastery again become a necessity of the national life : yet we must admit that in the ninth century Alfred had no more powerful weapon for the maintenance of a religious standard than the monastery.

In the cause of education, indeed, Alfred was before his age, and even before our age. He desired universal education. At his Court he pro-vided instructors for his children and the children of the nobles. They learned to read and write, they studied their own language and its poetry :

they learned Latin : and they learned what were
called the " liberal sciences," among them the art
of music.   But he thought also of the poorer
class.   "My desire," he says, "is that all the
freeborn youths of my people may persevere in
learning until they can perfectly read the English
Scriptures."   Unhappily he was unable to carry
out this wish.   Only in our own days has been at
last attempted the dream of the Saxon King—the
extension of education to the whole people.

One more aspect of Alfred's foresight.   He
endeavoured to remove the separation of his island
from the rest of the world : he connected his
people with the civilisation of Western Europe by
encouraging scholars and men of learning, workers
in gold, and craftsmen of all kinds, to come over :
he created commercial relations with foreign
countries : a merchant who made three voyages
to the Mediterranean he ennobled : he sent an
embassy every year to Rome : he sent an embassy
as far as India : he brought to bear upon
the somewhat sluggish minds of his people the
imagination and the curiosity which would here-
after engender a spirit of enterprise to which no
other nation can offer a parallel.

It was partly with this view that he strongly
enforced the connection with Rome.   One bond
of union the nations of the West should have—a
common Faith : and that defined and interpreted

for them by the same authority. Had it not been for that central authority the nations would have been divided, rather than drawn towards each other, by a Christianity split up into at least as many sects as there were languages. Imagine the evil, in an ignorant time, of fifty nations, each swearing by its own creed, and every creed different. From this danger Alfred kept his country free.

The last, not the least, of his achievements is that to Alfred we owe the foundations of our literature : the most noble literature that the world has ever seen. He collected and preserved the poetry based on the traditions and legends brought from the German Forests. He himself delighted to hear and to repeat these legends and traditions : the deeds of the mighty warriors who fought with monsters, dragons, wild boars, and huge serpents. He made his children learn their songs : he had them sung in his Court. The tradition goes that he could himself sing them to the music of his own harp. This wild and spontaneous poetry which Alfred preserved is the beginning of our own noble choir of poets. In other words, the foundation of that stately Palace of Literature, built up by our poets and writers for the admiration and instruction and consolation of mankind, was laid by Alfred. Well, but he did more than collect the poetry, he began the prose. Before Alfred there was no Anglo-Saxon prose.

I have already quoted Green's remark that in everything that Alfred designed or accomplished he put aside every personal aim or ambition in order to devote himself wholly to the welfare of those over whom he ruled. In his capacity as author this remark is specially illustrated. You all know that it is the leading characteristic—or the infirmity—of the poet, author, writer, to consider himself as part of his message. Alfred put himself aside : he presented his works in translations : they were, indeed, translations : but embellished, altered, enriched by his own work thus modestly presented. There is one book, now quite neglected, which for a thousand years profoundly moved the world of Western Europe. It is a book, written in prison by a noble Roman named Boethius, a philosopher, soldier, poet, and mathematician. It is entitled the *Consolation of Philosophy*. Fortunately the author, who wrote it from a prison, had time to finish it before they executed him. This book Alfred translated or imitated. For he filled his translations with his own thoughts and his own judgments. He gives his own theories of government : of the duties of a king : of maintaining the population, and especially the proper proportion of the different classes required to keep the nation in a state of efficiency. Every man in the country is a weapon which may be—and should be—used for the advancement of the general welfare. It is the king's duty to select the best instruments, and to use them to the best advantage. We even find brief notes of his own thoughts. "This," says the king, among these notes, "I can now truly say, that so long as I have lived I have striven to live worthily, and after my death to leave my memory to my descendants in good works."

It is not the part of this Introduction to dwell upon the whole of Alfred's literary work. It is enough if we recognise that he introduced education and restored learning. In the course of time, innumerable books were attributed to him : it is said that he translated the Psalms. A book of proverbs and sayings is attributed to him—each one begins with the words "Thus said Alfred." The Anglo-Saxon Chronicle and contemporary record of events is said to have been commenced by him. And since it is certain from the life of the king by one of his own Court that he was regarded by all classes of his people with the utmost reverence and respect, I think it is extremely likely that some of his people listened and took down in writing the sayings of the king, so that the book of Alfred's sayings may be as authentic as the sayings of Dr. Johnson, recorded by his admirer Boswell.

There is next to be observed the permanence of Alfred's institutions. They do not perish, but remain. His Witenagemot—Meeting of the Wise —is our Parliament—it has developed into our many Parliaments.   His order of King, Thane, and Freeman is our order of King, Lords, and Commons.   His theory of education was carried out in some of the towns, and in all the monasteries and cathedrals : there are schools still existing which owe their origin to a period before the Norman Conquest.   His foundation of all law upon the Laws of God remains our own : his liberties are our liberties : his navy is the ancestor of our navy : the literature which he planted has grown into a goodly tree—the Monarch of the Forest : the foreign trade that he began is the forerunner of our foreign trade : it would seem as if there was hardly any point in which we have reason to be grateful or proud which was not foreseen by this wise king.

To look for the secret of his wisdom is like looking for the secret of making a great poem or writing a great play : it may be arrived at and described, but it is not therefore the easier of imitation.   Alfred's secret is quite simple.   *His work was permanent because it was established on the national character.*   It was in order to make this point clear that I dwelt at length on the character of the people over whom Alfred ruled. He knew their character, and by instinct, which we call genius, he gave his people the laws and the education, and the power of development for which they were fitted.   No other laws, no other kind of government, will enable a people to prosper except those laws to which they have grown and are adapted. Only those institutions, I repeat, are permanent which are based on the national character. That was the secret of King Alfred the law-giver.

It may be asked, what manner of man to look at was this great king? His biographer, Asser, who knew him well, has not thought fit to tell us. He only says in words of flattery that Alfred was more comely and gracious of aspect than his brothers. These brothers, four in number, were all kings before him, and all died young. Alfred himself was afflicted by a disease which never left him. It is therefore presumable that there was some congenital weakness in them all. This was not physical weakness: whatever the disease, it did not interfere with Alfred's courage or his prowess in battle. This is proved by the fact that the Saxon kings actually fought in person in the forefront of the battle, and on foot. Alfred, for instance, fought in a dozen battles at least, and always with the valour that belongs to a strong man. I take him to have been a man of good stature and of strong build: a man whose appearance was kingly: who impressed his followers with the gallant and confident carriage of a brave soldier. But as to his face, or the colour of his hair or eyes, I can tell nothing. Fair hair he had,

I think, and blue eyes : or the more common type of brown hair and gray eyes. When a king resigns all personal ambitions and seeks nothing for himself, it seems natural and fitting that, while his works live after him, he himself should vanish without leaving so much as a tradition of his face or figure.

From time to time in history—generally in some time of great doubt and trouble : or in some time when the old ideals are in danger of being forgotten : or in some time when the nation seems losing the sense of duty and of responsibility : there appears one, man or woman, who restores the better spirit of the people by his example : by his preaching : by his self-sacrifice : by his martyr-dom. He is the prophet as priest : the prophet as king : the prophet as law-giver. There passes in imagination before us a splendid procession of men and women who have thus restored a nation or raised the fallen ideals. Among them we recognise many faces : there are Savonarola : Francis of Assisi : Joan of Arc : our own Queen Elizabeth, greatest and strongest of all women : the Czar Peter. But the greatest figure of them all—the most noble—the most god-like—is that of the ninth-century Alfred, king of that little country which you have upon your map. There is none like Alfred in the whole page of history : none with a record altogether so blameless : none so wise :

none so human. We have allowed the memory of him to be too much forgotten : only here and there a historian—such as Freeman or Green—lifts up his voice and proclaims aloud that he has no words with which to speak adequately of this great Englishman. Perhaps the noble lines of Tennyson, written for another prince whose memory is dear to us all, may be referred to Alfred :

> Who reverenced his conscience as his king ;
> Whose glory was, redressing human wrong ;
> Who spake no slander, no, nor listen'd to it ;
> Who loved one only and who clave to her—
> We know him now : we see him as he moved :
> How modest, kindly, all-accomplish'd, wise,
> With what sublime repression of himself ;
> Not making his high place the lawless perch
> Of wing'd ambitions, nor a vantage-ground
> For pleasure ; but thro' all this tract of years
> Wearing the white flower of a blameless life.

It is the purpose — the wise and patriotic purpose—of certain persons to erect, for these and other reasons, a monument, visible to all, to the memory of King Alfred.

Some of the points which I have recalled in this paper may help to show why such a monument would have been fitting at any time during the last thousand years. There is, however, a special reason which makes the erection of such a monument very necessary—I use the word necessary

advisedly—at the present time.   In the year 1897
—on that memorable day when we were all drunk
with the visible glory and the greatness of the
Empire—there arose in the minds of many a feeling
that we ought to teach the people the meaning of
what we saw set forth in that procession—the meaning of our Empire—not only what it is, but how it
came—through whose creation—by whose foundation.   Now so much is Alfred the Founder that
every ship in our Navy might have his name—
every school his bust : every Guildhall his statue.
He is everywhere.   But he is invisible.   And the
people do not know him.   The boys do not learn
about him.   There is nothing to show him.   We
want a monument to Alfred, if only to make the
people learn and remember the origin of our
Empire—if only that his noble example may be
kept before us, to stimulate and to inspire and to
encourage.

It seems unnecessary to urge that a monument
to Alfred must be set up in Winchester, and
not in London or in Westminster, or anywhere else.   Here lies the dust of the kings his
ancestors, and of the kings his successors.   Thirty-
five of his line made Winchester their capital :
twenty were buried in the Cathedral.   In this city
Alfred received instruction from St. Swithin : the
city was already old and venerable when Alfred
was a boy.   He was buried first in the Cathedral,

and afterwards in the Abbey, which he himself founded, hard by. The name of Alfred's country, well-nigh forgotten, except by scholars, has been revived of late years by a Wessex man—Thomas Hardy. But the name of Alfred's capital continues in the venerable and historic city of Winchester, which yields to none in England for the monuments and the memories of the past.

I venture, lastly, to express my own personal hope that great as were the achievements of Alfred —the keynote to be struck and to be maintained will be that Alfred is, and will always remain, the typical man of our race—call him Anglo-Saxon, call him American, call him Englishman, call him Australian—the typical man of our race at his best and noblest. I like to think that the face of the Anglo-Saxon at his best and noblest is the face of Alfred. I am quite sure and certain that the mind of the Anglo-Saxon at his best and noblest is the mind of Alfred: that the aspirations, the hopes, the standards of the Anglo-Saxon at his best and noblest are the aspirations, the hopes, the standards of Alfred. He is truly our Leader, our Founder, our King. When our monument takes shape and form let it somehow recognise this great, this cardinal fact. Let it show somehow by the example of Alfred the Anglo-Saxon at his best and noblest—here within the circle of the narrow seas, or across the ocean ; wherever King Alfred's language is spoken ; wherever King Alfred's laws prevail ; into whatever fair lands of the wide world King Alfred's descendants have penetrated.

WALTER BESANT.

ALFRED AS KING

By Frederic Harrison

ALFRED AS KING

T is a commonplace with historians—
and with the historians of many
countries and different schools of
opinion—that our English Alfred was
the only perfect man of action recorded in history ;
for Aurelius was occasionally too much of the philosopher ; Saint Louis usually too much of the saint ;
Godfrey too much of the Crusader ; the great
Emperors were not saints at all ; and of all more
modern heroes we know too much to pretend that
they were perfect. Of all the hyperboles of praise
there is but one that we can safely justify with the
strictest canons of historic research. Of all the
names in history there is only our English Alfred
whose record is without stain and without weakness—who is equally amongst the greatest of men
in genius, in magnanimity, in valour, in moral
purity, in intellectual force, in practical wisdom,
and in beauty of soul. In his recorded career
from infancy to death, we can find no single
trait that is not noble and suggestive, nor a

single act or word that can be counted as a flaw.

In the history of modern Europe there is nothing which can compare in duration and in organic continuity with the unbroken evolution of our English nation. And now that the royal house of France has passed from the sphere of political realities into that of historic memories, there is no dynasty in Europe which can be named in the same breath with that which has seen a succession of forty-nine sovereigns since Alfred ; nor has any King or Cæsar a record of ancestry which can compare with that of the royal Lady who through thirty-two generations traces her lineal descent to the Hero-King of Wessex.

We have long given up the venerable fables which once gathered round the name of Alfred, as round Romulus, or Theseus, King Arthur, or the Cid. Every schoolboy knows that Alfred was not formally King of all England ; nor did he introduce trial by jury, or electoral institutions ; he did not found the University of Oxford ; nor write all the pieces which are attributed to his pen ; he was perhaps too practical a man to let his own supper get burnt on the hearth ; and too wary a general to go about masquerading with a harp in the enemy's camp. But the historic Alfred whom we know to-day is a personage more splendid and lifelike than the legendary Alfred ever was.

Though much of what our grandsires believed about Alfred is now known to be poetry and pious fraud, the traditional Alfred was quite just in general effect, and modern research has given us a portrait both nobler and more definite than that drawn by the patriotic imagination of a less critical age. Patriotic imagination itself falls far short of scrupulous scholarship when it seeks to draw the likeness of a real hero.

It is true that the field of Alfred's achievements was relatively small, and the whole scale of his career was modest indeed when compared with that of his imperial compeers. He inherited a kingdom which covered only a few English counties, and at one time his realm was reduced to a smaller area than that of some private landlords of modern times. Beside the great Emperor Charles, or the German Ottos, Henrys, and Fredericks of the Middle Ages, his dominions, his resources, his armies, his battles, his fleets, his administrative machinery, his contemporary glory—all these were almost in miniature—hardly a tithe of theirs. But, we should remember, it is *quality* not *quantity* that weighs in the impartial scales of History. True human greatness needs no vast territories as its stage —nor do multitudes add to its power. That which tells in the end is the living seed of the creative mind, the heroic example, the sovereign gift of leadership, the undying inspiration of genius and faith.

Turn to the *Chronicle* and to Asser's *Life*, with recent historians and scholars, and mark those miracles of patience, valour, indomitable energy by which the great king rescued from the savage Norsemen the England of our forefathers. Watch him as he returns to the charge after every repulse, rallies his exhausted men, gathers up new armies, plans fresh methods of war, and at last wins for his people prosperity, honour, and peace. The scale of these campaigns was narrow—the armies were small —not indeed weaker than were the Greeks at Thermopylae and Marathon; but the annals of war have nothing grander than the long record of sagacious heroism by which Alfred saved England for the English. Then note the genius with which he saw that the Norsemen must be met on the sea, with which he organised a navy of ships built on a new design of his own. Alfred is not only the forerunner of Marlborough and Wellington, but he was the first to teach the Saxon to be a seaman.

A fine land that had once known prosperity, and even culture, lay utterly ruined and desolate when Alfred undertook the vast task of its restoration—its material, moral, intellectual reform. He said in his Will, "we were all despoiled by the Heathen Folk." He found the enemy in possession of something like a standing army of disciplined soldiers; and we should note how the

Chronicle calls the Norsemen "the army." He met this by instituting a regular militia with local garrisons and a reserve force capable of systematic war. When Alfred marshals a new campaign we find that the era of wild raids to be met by casual musters of countrymen is a thing of the past. Alfred at last has his "army" too. We are dealing with regular armies capable of sustaining organised campaigns.

A navy needed to be created and not simply reformed. And the safety of the southern shores of England—the first command of the Channel—must be dated from the day when Alfred began the formation of an adequate fleet. It is true that in the absence of competent seamen in Wessex, he had to man his earliest ships with Frisians from over the sea. But in later years he came to have a really English fleet of his own. And it is plain that in a true sense he is the inventor, but not the actual founder, of a national navy : of that sea-power which is the birthright of this island.

When Alfred was chosen king, " almost against his will," we are told, the prospect was one to appal the stoutest heart. In his boyhood the Northmen had begun to winter in Kent, had taken Canterbury and London by storm, and pushed up the Thames. A few years later they stormed Winchester and ravaged Kent. In the reign of his brother, Ethelred, they stormed York, and

invaded Mercia, whose king, Burhred, had married
Alfred's sister.　They next laid waste East Anglia,
martyred its king, Edmund, and threatened
Wessex.　The Danes (as they were now known)
sailed up the Thames, and formed a camp round
Reading.　In a fierce battle at Ashdown a victory
had been won for the moment by the energy and
valour of Alfred ; but defeats followed, Surrey
was lost, and Ethelred died, it is supposed of his
wounds.

The young king of twenty-two came to the
throne of his ancestors in a dark hour.　The
supremacy of Wessex in England, won by his
grandfather, Egbert, had vanished.　Northumbria,
Mercia, East Anglia, and parts of Wessex had
been desolated ; the abbeys had been sacked, the
monks murdered, the churches, schools, and home-
steads ruined.　The Danish invaders were masters
of all Northern, Eastern, and Central England,
and the heart of Wessex was open to assault.
The young king met them at Wilton with a small
force, but after a stubborn fight was beaten off.
He was forced to purchase a precarious truce.

In this year, 871, the *Chronicle* relates (in its
grim, laconic style), the [Danish] army came to
Reading, and three nights after, the Alderman
Ethelwulf fought them.　Four nights after this,
Ethelred and Alfred led a large force to Reading,
and "there was great slaughter on both sides ;

the Alderman Ethelwulf was slain, and the Danes held possession of the battle place." "And four nights after, Ethelred and Alfred fought with all the army at Ashdown"; many thousands were slain; "and they were fighting until night." And fourteen nights after, King Ethelred and Alfred his brother fought against the army at Basing, and there the Danes gained the victory. "And two months after, King Ethelred and Alfred his brother fought against the army at Merton . . . and there was great slaughter on each side, but the Danes held possession of the battle place. And after this fight there came a great summer force [of Danes] to Reading. And the Easter after, King Ethelred died. Then Alfred his brother succeeded to the kingdom of the West Saxons, and one month after, with a small force, he fought against all the army at Wilton, but the Danes held possession of the battle place. *And this year nine great battles were fought against the army in the kingdom south of the Thames; besides which Alfred, the king's brother, and individual aldermen, and king's thanes, often rode raids on them, which were not reckoned."*

Such were the disasters with which Alfred's reign began. His fighting-men were exhausted or slaughtered; his kingdom torn from side to side, and its chief towns stormed : the northern, central, and eastern kingdoms had been blotted out.

Burhred of Mercia was driven over sea, and Wessex was forced to buy a brief rest with gold. Alfred equipped a few ships and gained some temporary success. But soon after, the Danes with a great fleet swept round the south coast and penetrated into Dorsetshire and Devonshire. Thence passing northwards into Gloucestershire, and reinforced by a new fleet in the Bristol Channel, the Danish host suddenly fell upon Wiltshire. The Saxon defence was broken in pieces. "The [Danish] army harried the West Saxons' land, and settled there, and drove over sea much of the people, and of the rest the most they harried. *And the people submitted to them, save the King Alfred; and he, with a little band, withdrew to the woods and fastnesses in the moors.*"

Alfred seemed utterly ruined. He, the grandson of Egbert overlord of England, the successor on the throne of Wessex of his father and his three brothers, had been king just seven years, and in scores of battles he had been fighting the Danes for ten years. He had seen the three northern kingdoms of Angles broken up and the reigning house in each exterminated. Step by step he had seen Kent, Surrey, and Wessex overrun; assailed by sea and land, from the coast, the rivers, and the Bristol Channel. His own people had been driven across sea, or crushed into submission; and he himself, with a small band of followers, was forced to find shelter in woods and swamps. His lot seemed hopeless, but he alone did not despair.

The crisis was indeed the gravest to which our country has ever been exposed. The Danish host was now a large and disciplined army bent on conquering and settling new lands, and already masters of the island from the Severn to the Tees. They were the fiercest and rudest of the tribes which had broken into Europe ; Heathens, full of hatred and scorn for the religion, culture, arts, and civilisation of Christendom. With a real genius for war, both by sea and land, fired with the thirst of glory and adventure, they were better armed, more mobile, more martially organised than Saxon, Angle, or Jute. Short of a miracle their ultimate triumph over the whole island seemed certain. Had it been achieved, the civilisation of England would have been retarded for ages. Christianity, learning, arts, and legislation, which had progressed for two centuries, would have been stamped out, and our island would have been the seat of a barbarous and heathen horde. From the nature of their island conquest and their own mastery of the seas, they could not have been absorbed in Christendom so rapidly as were the Normans of France, or the Danubian tribes of Germany. They might have resisted for centuries both conversion and conquest from Europe. Nay more, from the supreme opportunities afforded by our island and all its resources as a basis for an imperial race, it is too probable that the heathen Danes, once firmly seated in the whole of Britain, might have proved the lasting scourge of Europe itself. From this tremendous peril, England and Europe were saved by the genius of our Saxon hero.

In the Easter of that year, 878, the *Chronicle* relates, " Alfred, with a little band, wrought a fortress at Athelney, and from that work warred on the army, with that portion of the men of Somerset that was nearest." Athelney was a bit of firm ground in the morasses formed by the Parret and the Tone in Somersetshire. There, for a few months, the king organised a new army, drawn from Somerset and Wilts and such Hants men as were left. In May he suddenly dashed out of the wood of Selwood : " his Wessex men were rejoiced to see him " : he fought a great fight against the whole " army " at Ethandune, near Westbury, put them to flight and drove them to their camp, where, after fourteen days of siege, he forced the Danes to surrender. It was a crushing victory—the turning-point in the life of Alfred— in the life of England.

The importance of it was this. A part of the beaten host sailed away over seas. But the rest, under their king, Guthrum, agreed to accept Christian baptism, to withdraw out of Wessex and the western half of Mercia, and to settle peaceably in East Anglia, north of Thames. Guthrum, with thirty of his chiefs, came to Alfred's stronghold, received at his baptism the Saxon name of Athelstan from his victor and god-father, remained twelve days with the king and gave large presents. By the Peace of Wedmore, 878, Wessex and West England were saved, and the ultimate incorporation of the Danes with Christendom was secured. At first sight and in strict form, Alfred had surrendered Eastern England to the conqueror. The Treaty was not honestly observed by the Danes, and Guthrum and his warriors again became enemies. But the core of England was saved ; the amalgamation of Dane and Saxon was founded in principle and in distant effect. And the Peace of Wedmore was a stroke of genius more daring and more far-reaching in result than the splendid victory of Ethandune by which it had been won.

Leaving the Danes for the present undisturbed in all Eastern England between Thames and Tees, Alfred occupied himself with restoring his shattered and desolated Kingdom of Wessex. His treasury was empty, the towns were in ruins, and civil government paralysed. He built forts, abbeys, and schools ; repeopled and stocked waste districts ; and set to work to establish something like a standing military force to meet the regular "army" of Danes. Hitherto Alfred had commanded loose levies of half-armed men, who by custom disbanded after two months' service. This had enabled small but organised bands of Danes to overrun England, and to win practical successes even when beaten by numbers in the fields. Alfred, like William of Normandy in the eleventh, like Cromwell in the seventeenth century, saw, even so early as the ninth century, that victory belonged not to numbers but to regular armies. He organised what was at least a permanent local militia, with definite quotas of levies and an alternate system of reserves, besides the garrisons of fortified places. He rebuilt the broken fortresses, exercised his men in entrench-ments, and adapted from the Danes their military arts.

But his eye of genius foresaw that the country was not safe whilst the invaders had command of the seas. Thus he organised a fleet, and assessed the ports and maritime districts to support it. He himself ultimately designed a class of ship, longer and swifter than those in use, though at first he had to man his navy with mercenary Frisians and sea-rovers. Towards the close of his reign, and in that of his son and grandson, a genuine English navy asserted its command of the Channel, which two centuries later his feeble successors lost again.

He then turned to reorganise the system of justice, making the judges the direct ministers of the sovereign, personally responsible to him, and subject in certain cases to his final appeal. His biographer tells us that he keenly revised unjust judgments, and tradition exaggerated this into a preposterous legend. He caused a collection of the old laws to be compiled—carefully resisting any general new legislation, or the fusion of the Wessex, Mercian, and Kentish customs into a symmetrical code. His laws were a compilation, with selection of what was approved best, and rejection of what was condemned as obsolete or mischievous. In the spirit of conservative amendment which marks his whole career, he is careful to tell us that he "durst not venture to set down much of his own." He was content with partial revision and excision, under the advice of his Witan.

The combination in a code of Saxon, Anglian, and Kentish "dooms" gave a certain stimulus towards national union in a larger aggregate. But a much more powerful cause unexpectedly emerged out of the Danish invasions. By these savage shocks the royal houses that had ruled in Mercia, in East Anglia, in Northumbria, were not only overthrown, but were extinct. Alfred remained the one victorious king of the race of Cerdic, the legitimate sovereign of Wessex and Kent, the natural source of kingly authority wherever Danes were not in possession of rule. Having won back the western half of Mercia by the Peace of Wedmore, Alfred became its king by silent consent of

its Anglian people.   He did not fuse West Mercia
with Wessex ; he was not formally installed or
crowned.   He made Ethelred, the husband of his
daughter Ethelfleda, alderman, and himself exercised the functions of king, with a separate Mercian
administration and Witan.   By this wise and tenta-
tive system of dual monarchy, Alfred was firmly
seated the undisputed sovereign of Southern England from the mouth of the Thames to the Exe,
ruling by his son-in-law all Central England west
of Watling Street from the Severn to the Ribble.
He thus became, but a few years after his romantic
sortie from Athelney, the most powerful ruler
holding the widest single realm within our island.
This effected a practical supremacy over the main
part of England proper, except for the Danes in
the east.   And he thus made it possible that there
should be a true English kingdom, of which his
son Edward, and his grandson Athelstan, were
formally recognised as sovereigns.

More than once after the settlement effected at
Wedmore and the years of peace it brought, Alfred
had to meet formidable enemies both by sea and
land.   But fierce as these campaigns were, they
did not imply such incessant warfare, such desperate
crises, as had made the first ten years of his early
manhood one long battle for life and home.   Alfred
was now at least as well able to defend his country
from the Scandinavian invaders as were the rulers

of France and Germany, on whom the storm burst whenever the Northmen had been checked in England.

Six years after the Peace of Wedmore Alfred had to meet again a force of Danes which had pushed up the Thames, and to chastise the East Anglians who had violated the Treaty by a fresh outbreak. A new treaty with Guthrum gave Alfred possession of London and adjacent parts of Middlesex, which were finally rescued from the Danes, and annexed to English Mercia under its alderman, Ethelred, Alfred's son-in-law. Again, in the twenty third year of Alfred's reign a new body of Vikings from Norway descended on to Wessex and were joined by a second rising of the Anglian Danes. For more than two years the war was continued over a large part of England— from the Thames and its affluents across to the Severn ; from Exeter northwards to Chester. By a series of vigorous and skilful campaigns, in concerted strategy of armies and fleets, the king, his son and his son-in-law, defeated this formidable combination, captured the entire Danish fleet, overawed the Britons of Wales and Cornwall, forced the East Anglian Danes to keep within their own reserves, and drove the northern freebooters across the Channel. Once again, in the last years of his reign, Alfred had to meet a new invasion of pirates at sea, who were defeated in a series of fierce and bloody encounters. These are the last recorded campaigns of the king, who from his boyhood, for nearly thirty years, had been continually in arms ; but, by obstinate wars and sagacious policy, he had tamed the savage Norsemen, and at length transmitted to his descendants a kingdom doubled and trebled in extent and greatly increased in culture and strength.

England had been rescued from barbarism by the heroism of Alfred and his aptitude for war. But it is his genius as a creative statesman which left permanent effects on the history of England and made him one of the principal founders of the greatness of our country. His conversion and settlement of Guthrum's Danes in East Anglia, his generous forbearance and his repeated treaties with them in spite of their faithless conduct, led to the ultimate amalgamation of Dane, Angle, and Saxon, which created the compound English race. A less sagacious victor would have sought to clear his country of Norsemen, and would undoubtedly have been overwhelmed by successive invasions himself. Alfred's whole career shows a conscious purpose to break with the tribal and local isolation of the West Saxon, to attach Wessex with Mercia, to civilise Dane and Briton, and to bring England into closer union with the religious and political system of Europe.

Alfred's restoration of London was the stroke of a true statesman. The city had been stormed by the Norsemen in 851, and since then had been desolate and almost deserted, save when occupied by the Danes as winter-quarters, as it was in 872. Within the Danish power it remained until 886, the year of Alfred's second treaty with Guthrum. By that it was ceded to him with the adjacent part of Middlesex. The king rebuilt its walls and repeopled it, and added it to Mercia, from which it was not again separated. The military and political genius of Alfred and his long experience of war with the Danes had seized on the immense importance of a restored London, carved out of Danish East Anglia, with power to block all incursions up the Thames and its various tributary rivers. The restoration of London by the King of Wessex was thus an epoch in the history, not only of the city itself, but of the country of which it was destined by nature to be the capital.

Alfred had been at this date fifteen years on the throne, and the whole aspect of affairs was changed. When he began to reign heathen barbarians were masters of the Eastern, Central, and Northern parts of England, and threatened to break up Wessex. They swept round all coasts, and pushed up the rivers, plundering, burning, raiding, and slaughtering. Now, they were shut up in East Anglia, outwardly christianised, bound by formal treaties of peace, confronted at sea by strong fleets, and gradually submitting to the moral force of superior civilisation. As Goths and Franks were overawed by the Roman empire they conquered, so Vikings and Danes gradually recognised the higher organisation of Wessex. Alfred at last ruled over a compact realm stretching from the Channel up to the Ribble, with fortresses in such places as Rochester, London, Exeter, and Chester. Lastly, in a rebuilt London, he was master of the Thames, with a powerful base on the Danish side of the great river.

As Alfred, we are told, was at Rome in his sixth year, and had subsequently been with his father at the Court of Charles the Bald, whose daughter Judith became the boy's step-mother, the young king must have been impressed by his memories of foreign lands. His yearly embassies with offerings to the Pope, and the restoration of the Saxon College at Rome, bear witness to his close relations with the See. He married his own daughter, Elfrida, to Baldwin II., Count of Flanders, son of the same Judith, and ancestor of Matilda, wife of the Conqueror. This brought about a connection between England and Flanders, both so much threatened by Northmen invaders.

With the Britons of Cornwall and Wales Alfred's policy showed the same moderation, sagacity, and practical skill. They were not dangerous unless united and in active combination with Danes. By the creation of English Mercia, he effectively cut them off from East Anglia ; and his whole policy was directed to detach them by separate tribes and to win them into peaceful union with his own people. He had to fight them in groups from time to time, but he never attempted to conquer or annex them in the mass. And after the failure of the house of Roderick, of North Wales, Alfred secured a recognised supremacy over both North and South Welsh. His wise, firm, and victorious government impressed the smaller and more backward tribes on all sides; so that, without demanding any formal subjection, his paramount authority was recognised over the island, whilst his sphere of influence was extended to Northumbrians and Scots. The defence and reorganisation of Wessex had founded a sentiment of national unity, which was ultimately to be con- solidated in a formal kingdom of all England. He made Wessex an organic, civilised, and pro- gressive kingdom, and created it as the type which England was to follow.

It was the same idea of bringing England into the European world which suggested Alfred's very remarkable series of distant voyages and missions. The characteristic account of the discoveries of Ohthere and Wulfstan round the North Cape and in the Baltic, which Alfred inserts into his translation of *Orosius*, testifies to the king's strong interest in the geography and ethnography of Europe. The expedition which he despatched to India, it is said, in 883, to the shrines of St. Thomas and St. Bartholomew, in accordance with his vow when he recovered London from the Danes, was a really extraordinary feat for that age ; and, though some of the MSS. read *Judea* for *India*, it is thought that the mission was really sent to Christian churches then known to exist in India. Asser relates that the king received letters and presents from the patriarch of Jerusalem ; a tale which the later writers considerably embellish. A deep impression was left by Alfred's zeal to extend his foreign relations with distant lands.

His policy of calling in men of learning, teachers, ecclesiastics, and seamen from countries outside his own, is more fully recorded. Asser, the learned and excellent monk of St. David's, was brought out of Wales and pressed into the service of the king, whose friend, counsellor, and biographer he became. Plegmund was brought out of Mercia and made Archbishop of Canterbury ; another Mercian, Werfrith, Bishop of Worcester, was the constant adviser of the king, both in literary and in state affairs. Grimbald was brought from the monastery of St. Omer ; and John, of Saxony, from the monastery of Corbey. With these came learned monks to organise the new abbeys and schools

which Alfred founded. He encouraged foreign
traders, and summoned artists and craftsmen from
the Continent to direct his buildings and arts.
Until his Saxons had learned seamanship, he engaged Frisians to man his ships, and took into his
service adventurous Vikings such as Ohthere and
Wulfstan.

Alfred has left us his own conception of what a
king should be : and no preacher or moralist has
ever drawn the portrait in grander lines :—

Power is never a good, unless he be good that has it ;
so it is the good of the man, not of the power. If power
be goodness, therefore is it that no man by his dominion
can come to the virtues, and to merit ; but by his virtues
and merit he comes to dominion and power. Thus no
man is better for his power ; but if he be good, it is from
his virtues that he is good. From his virtues he becomes
worthy of power, if he be worthy of it. . . . By wisdom
you may come to power, though you should not desire the
power. You need not be solicitous about power, nor
strive after it. If you be wise and good, it will follow
you, though you should not wish it.

Ah ! Wise One, thou knowest that greed and the
possession of this earthly power never were pleasing to me,
nor did I ever greatly desire this earthly kingdom—save
that I desired tools and materials to do the work that
it was commanded me to do. This was that I might
guide and wield wisely the authority committed to me.
Why ! thou knowest that no man may understand any
craft or wield any power, unless he have tools and
materials. Every craft has its proper tools. But the

tools that a king needs to rule are these : to have his land fully peopled ; to have priestmen, and soldiermen, and workmen. Yea ! thou knowest that without these tools no king can put forth his capacity to rule. . . . It was for this I desired materials to govern with, that my ability to rule might not be forgotten and hidden away. For every faculty and authority is apt to grow obsolete and ignored, if it be without wisdom ; and that which is done in unwisdom can never be reckoned as skill. *This will I say—that I have sought to live worthily the while I lived, and after my life to leave to the men that come after me a remembering of me in good works.*

    .   .   .   .   .

Ah ! my soul, one evil is stoutly to be shunned. It is that which most constantly and grievously deceives all those who have a nature of distinction, but who have not attained to full command of their powers. This is the desire of false glory and of unrighteous power, and of immoderate fame of good deeds above all other people. For many men desire power that they may have fame, though they be unworthy, for even the most depraved desire it also. But he that will investigate this fame wisely and earnestly, will perceive how little it is, how precarious, how frail, how bereft it is of all that is good.

Glory of this world ! Why do foolish men with a false voice call thee glory ? Thou art not so. More men have pomp and glory and worship from the opinion of foolish people, than they have from their own works.

They say a certain king cried : he had a naked sword hanging over his head by a small thread ready at a moment to cut short his life. It was so always to me. . . .

Alfred's relations to the Church were wholly without a cloud or a blot—alike free from the violence or the impolicy which too often discredited even the noblest sovereigns of his age. From the hour when the child Prince of four was anointed by Pope Leo in Rome, down to the day when the Canons laid his bones in the Old Minster of Winchester, the career of Alfred presents to us the purest type of the normal relations between the temporal and spiritual powers—a type of more wisdom than that of St. Henry or St. Louis, more truly spiritual than that of the Emperors Charles or Otto. To Alfred, Religion, Culture, Intelligence had no local limits. He was essentially European, even cosmopolitan, in his genius. As a boy he had witnessed the inauguration of the new Papal Rome on the Vatican. He had been at the Court of the great Frank King, whose daughter became his step-mother ; he had known all that was foremost in the civilisation of the century : he resolved to transplant it to England. His missions were his message to the world that Britain was no longer an *ultima Thule*, but henceforth was to march in the van of Progress. He was, says Freeman, "the spiritual and intellectual leader of his people."

It is in his own writings that we come to love Alfred best. No ruler of men has left us so pellucid a revelation of his own soul. As in

Meditations of Aurelius and the Psalms of David, there is given to men the outpourings of his aspirations and his sorrows. Neither Richelieu, Cromwell, nor William the Silent ever recorded more frankly their problems and their aims. In the authentic writings of Alfred we are in the presence of one who is a teacher as much as a king—who recalls to us Augustine and à-Kempis, or Bunyan and Jeremy Taylor. His *Boethius* served him as texts whereon he preached to his people profound sermons on the moral and spiritual life. Read his homily on Riches—" that it is better to give than to receive,"—on the true Ruler—" that power is never a good, unless he be good that has it,"—on the uses of Adversity — " no wise man should desire a soft life." Few men ever had so hard a life—with his mysterious and cruel malady—" his thorn in the flesh " until his early death—with his distracted and ruined kingdom — his ferocious enemies—his never-ending cares. And amidst it all we have the king in his silent study pouring out poetic thoughts upon married love, or friendship, on true happiness, or the inner life, composing pastoral poetry, or casting into English old idylls from Greek epic or myth, ending with some magnificent *Te Deum* of his own composition.

And with all this spiritual fervour, this literary genius, this passion for culture, how wonderful is the many-sided energy of the man—his skill and delight as a huntsman, his love of ballad, anecdote, and merry tale, his love of all noble art, his zeal as a great builder, his ingenuity in mechanical contrivance, his invention for measuring time, his planning a new type of battleship—his supreme foresight in refounding the desolated city of London. No man ever so perfectly fulfilled the rule—"Without haste, without rest." "I have desired," he wrote, "to live worthily while I lived, and after my life to leave to the men that should be after me a remembrance in good works." And Alfred "the truth-teller"—as an annalist calls him—never uttered words more true.

Alfred's name is almost the only one in the long roll of our national worthies which awakens no bitter, no jealous thought, which combines the honour of all ; Alfred represents at once the ancient monarchy, the army, the navy, the law, the literature, the poetry, the art, the enterprise, the industry, the religion of our race. Neither Welshman, nor Scot, nor Irishman can feel that Alfred's memory has left the trace of a wound for his national pride. No difference of Church arises to separate any who would join to do Alfred honour. No saint in the Calendar was a more loyal and cherished member of the ancient faith ; and yet no Protestant can imagine a purer and more simple follower of the Gospel. Alfred was a victorious warrior whose victories have left no curses behind them : a king whom no man ever charged with a harsh act : a scholar who never became a pedant : a saint who knew no superstition : a hero as bold as Launcelot —as spotless as Galahad.

No people, in ancient or modern times, ever had a hero-founder at once so truly historic, so venerable, and so supremely great. Alfred was more to us than the heroes in antique myths— more than Theseus and Solon were to Athens, or Lycurgus to Sparta, or Romulus and Numa were to Rome—more than St. Stephen was to Hungary, or Pelayo and the Cid to Spain—more than Hugh Capet and Jeanne d'Arc were to France—more than William the Silent was to Holland—nay, almost as much as the Great Charles was to the Franks.

The life-work of the Great Alfred has had a continuity, an organic development, a moral, intellectual, and spiritual majesty which has no parallel or rival amongst rulers in the annals of mankind. He is the father of English History, the founder of English prose. He gave impulse and form to the *English Chronicle*, the oldest national record in modern Europe. He formed himself, or dictated, an organic prose literature, which was kept in current use until the Norman Conquest. His mark as a king is the creative mind—the organising genius. His whole life, as recorded in act and as imagined in his own ideals, has the stamp of supreme insight, practical wisdom, self-control, devotion to duty. His passion for poetry, his love for history, his dignity, his grace, his tenderness, his manly piety—all alike are spontaneous and beautiful—all are in harmony, none are in excess.

ALFRED AS A RELIGIOUS MAN AND AN EDUCATIONALIST

By the Bishop of Bristol

ALFRED AS A RELIGIOUS MAN AND AN EDUCATIONALIST

I

HIS EARLY YEARS

Earliest years—Visits to Rome—Purpose of such visits—His father's will — His education — Saxon poetry — His mother's book—His religious interest—His desire for learning — Musical skill — His religious wars — He becomes king.

THE original sources of information from which this chapter is drawn are fairly numerous. Asser's *Life of Alfred* is of course the chief source; but Alfred's laws, Alfred's translations, Alfred's will, all throw much light on his character as a religious man ; and the translations tell us something of his views on education, besides what we learn from the record of his actions.

Alfred's mother was Osburga ; Asser tells us that she was a very religious woman, noble alike in family and by her own disposition.   His father Ethelwulf gave him an early training in devotion to the faith of Christ. In the year 853, which Asser declares to have been the fifth year of Alfred's life—though some say his eleventh year, which would seem more probable—Ethelwulf sent him to Rome with an honourable escort of nobles and commoners. Pope Leo IV. received him, anointed him for king, and adopted him as his spiritual son. This may mean that Alfred was confirmed in Rome; Ethelwerd, a descendant of Alfred, believed that it referred to baptism. Another account states that the Pope anointed him king of the Demetians; but that seems out of the question, as he had four brothers older than himself. The statement may be due to the fact that some years after Alfred became king, the kings and people of that part of Wales made submission to him.[1] Two years later Ethelwulf himself went to Rome, with great honour, and took with him Alfred, because he loved him more than his other sons. A long list of Ethelwulf's gifts was given by Anastasius in his *Lives of the Popes;* they were very magnificent if the record is true. The father

---

[1] We still have, at Llantwit Major, the beautiful monument set up by one of the kings who thus made submission, Howel, son of Ris. The Latin is not as good as the decoration of the monument : *ni nomine di patris et spiritus santdi anc crucem houelt properabit pro anima res patris eus.* The monument is a singularly beautiful "wheel" cross with broad stem. It has long been broken in two. It lies on the ground in the remarkable western portion of the double church at Llantwit.

and son remained in Rome for a year. Alfred's mother was, we must suppose, then dead, for Ethelwulf took a new wife home with him, Judith, the daughter of Charles the Bald.

We have in Ethelwulf's will an interesting evidence of the impression made upon him by Rome. It is as well to state such of the provisions as have come down to us, for they are in themselves of importance, and they introduce us to important facts of the time ; also, we shall then have something with which to compare Alfred's will when the time comes to deal with it. The provisions show the kind of religious atmosphere in which Alfred was brought up as a young boy.

Ethelwulf ordered that the money he left behind him should be divided between his sons and the nobles for the good of his soul. Further, for the benefit of his soul, which from the first flower of his youth he had studied in all things to promote, he directed that in all his hereditary dominions one poor man for each ten hides of land, either a native or a foreigner,[1] should be provided with meat, drink, and clothing, by his successors, even to the day of judgment. And the curiously significant condition is imported, " if the country should continue to be inhabited by men and cattle, and not become deserted " : to such an extent had the ravages of the Danish pirates

---

[1] Possibly meaning an Englishman who was not a Wessex man.

gone. Also, and still for the good of his soul,
three hundred mancuses[1] were to go to Rome.
Their destination explains to us the religious
attraction which drew men in his time to the old
capital of the Western world. The journey was
dangerous ;[2] it was also expensive.[3] King Canute
spoke very strongly about this in his time. He
thanked God that he had been able to visit the holy
Apostles Peter and Paul. That was the aspect in
which the purpose of the pilgrimage to Rome presented itself to his mind, it was to visit the tombs
of the holy Apostles Peter and Paul.[4] But having
thanked God for his visit, he proceeded to complain
of the heavy demands upon " my archbishops "
when according to custom they visited the holy see
to receive the pall. " I complained in the presence
of the lord Pope, and said I was much displeased
on account of the immense sums of money which
were demanded of them " ; it was decreed that this
should cease. In like manner he settled with

[1] The mancus was more than the third of a pound.

[2] In 959, Alfsin, Archbishop of Canterbury, died in the Alps on his way
for the pall, overcome by the snow and the cold.

[3] A hundred years before Alfred's time, Alcuin of York wrote to Bishop
Remedius of Coire, to beg him to let his messenger pass through the mountains to Italy without payment of the heavy tolls.

[4] Canute's descriptive letter is given by Florence, under the year 1031.
The argument used by Wilfrith at Whitby, and by Aldhelm in writing to
the Britons, had been brought to bear on the king. " I learned from wise
men that the holy Apostle Peter received of the Lord great power of binding
and loosing, and is the key-bearer of the heavenly kingdom, and thus I held it
mightily useful to seek diligently his more special patronage with the Lord."

the emperor and with the Frank king that the severity of the taxes by the way should be relaxed. In 688 and 728, two of Alfred's predecessors, Cædwalla and Ina, kings of Wessex, wishing to visit Rome, resigned their kingdom to carry out their wish. Bede tells us precisely what their purpose was. It was that they might visit the tombs of the blessed Apostles. Ethelwulf, too, makes his object clear in his will. One hundred mancuses were to go to Rome in honour of St. Peter, specially to buy oil for filling all the lamps of his apostolic church on Easter Eve and at cock-crow ; also, one hundred mancuses in honour of St. Paul, for the same purpose of providing oil for the Church of St. Paul the Apostle, to fill the lamps on Easter Eve and at cock-crow ; and one hundred mancuses for the universal apostolic pontiff. William of Malmesbury states that these were to be annual gifts, but that is not supported by Asser, from whom William takes his account.

It is interesting to note the agreement of these gifts with the facts of the time. In 847 the Saracens had attacked Rome. The great basilicas of St. Peter and St. Paul were suburban churches, outside the walls, and they were plundered and desecrated. We are accustomed to the idea of St. Paul's being *fuori le mura*, but St. Peter's, as we know it, lies in a district surrounded by walls.

This fortified district is called the Leonine City. It owes its existence and its name to Leo IV., who was Pope when Ethelwulf sent Alfred to Rome as a boy. A concise account of the eight years' papacy of Leo IV. would state that he devoted himself to building the fortifications of the Leonine City, that St. Peter's and the Vatican might no longer be suburban, and to restoring the plundered and desecrated churches of the two Apostles. Hence Ethelwulf's gifts to the two churches and the papal purse. If the dates and periods given by Asser are correct, Pope Leo died while the Saxon king and prince were in Rome, and was succeeded by Benedict III. In that case Alfred witnessed in the autumn of 855 the significant spectacle of an antipope stripping the Pope of his pontifical robes and ruling for a time in the Lateran.

Under influences such as these Alfred was brought up. His brothers appear to have been sent out to great men of the kingdom to be educated, but Alfred was kept always at the king's court, as the favourite son. He was specially noted for the attention with which he listened to the Saxon poems of earlier times, and the care with which he stored them up in an excellent memory. In after years he spoke of Aldhelm's English songs and hymns as the best he knew;[1] and

[1] We learn this from William of Malmesbury, Aldhelm's own monastery. William reports Alfred as saying that no one in any age equalled Aldhelm

that was saying a great deal, for the national gift of song, both sacred and secular, was great. It would be difficult to find in the early records of any nation a sacred song more touching and beautiful than the stanzas of the " Dream of the Holy Rood," incised in early Anglian runes upon the great cross-shaft at Ruthwell, itself a monument such as no other nation can show. The fuller form of this great song, embodying the earlier stanzas found on the Ruthwell cross, was discovered at Vercelli two generations ago, in the Wessex dialect of Alfred's time. That Alfred knew by heart this among many other English songs may be taken as certain. That it made its religious mark on his mind cannot be doubted.

But, Asser remarks with a severe comment on the neglect in this respect by his parents, the boy Alfred had no book-learning at all. He was trained in all bodily exercises, and he especially learned and practised the art of hunting in all its branches with surprising success ; an art so practical then that Asser believed skill and good fortune in hunting to be " among the gifts of God, as we have often witnessed." But book-learning he had none.

It was his mother who gave him his first taste for book-learning. If we are to accept the dates

in poetry, for he could make a poem, compose an air, and aptly either sing or recite. A street-song common in Alfred's time was composed by Aldhelm. See also p. 81.

and statements of Asser as on the whole correct, this must have been his step-mother, Judith, though one of the statements would refer it to Osburga's time. Alfred was about thirteen when the event occurred; he remained illiterate, Asser says, till he was twelve years old or more. Those who take the other view make him almost four at the time of the following episode. There is no evidence that Osburga had any learning, though her love for Saxon ballad may be assumed. Judith, on the other hand, was the daughter of a house which paid much regard to learning and art. The beautiful Bibles of her father are in existence still, and we can well understand that she would try to win the affection of her step-sons by showing them treasures of a kind new to them. No one who has had the privilege of handling and examining the books in the Bibliothèque Nationale in Paris can ever forget the beauty of the manuscripts which belonged to Charles le Chauve, Judith's father. The ivory covers of his Psalter and his Book of the Gospels, the beauty of the interior of those books, and the fineness of his St. Denis Bible and his Metz Bible (which is possibly the Bible prepared at Tours for Charlemagne under the care of Alcuin), abundantly convince us of the artistic taste of his family. Their evidence could be largely supplemented from the still-existing manuscripts of Charlemagne, Louis le Débonnaire, and Lothaire.

His mother, then, one day showed to Alfred and an older brother an ornamental manuscript of Saxon poems. To tempt them to begin to learn —again the act of one who had not been responsible for their ignorance of book-learning — she said she would give the book to the boy who could first learn to read it. Alfred was delighted with the beauty of the initial letter. He might well be delighted if it approached the beauty of the Lindisfarne gospels, wrought a century and a half before, or the very different style of beauty of the manuscript known as the Psalter of Athelstane, with its Byzantine type and Teutonic origin, parts of which Judith may well have seen and handled. The initial letter of the first Psalm in this Psalter would indeed have been a prize for which a boy might face the pain of learning to read, even a boy devoted to hunting.

Alfred spoke first, though the younger. "Will you really give it to the one who can most quickly understand and recite it before you?" She, glad and smiling, said, "To him I will give it." He took it from her hand, went to his master and read it. When it was read, he brought it back and recited it. It is not at all improbable that Judith did not know of his power of memory, and that instead of learning to read it, in our sense of the word, he got his master to read it over till he knew it by heart and could point with his finger to the words as he recited them. John the Deacon, writing in the same century, said that Pope Gregory the Great (others ascribe it to Gregory III.) invented musical notation as a *memoria technica* to remind him of tunes he had learned by ear.

However that might be with Alfred, he had got the taste for written words, which never left him. He set to work to learn the daily course of the religious services of the several hours ; and then certain of the psalms ; and then a number of prayers. All this collection he had in a little book which he carried day and night in his bosom. Asser, who joined him many years later, often saw him use this little book to assist his prayers, amid all the bustle and business of a king's life. But still there is a hint that when this collection was made it was only to him a representation of what he knew by heart ; for Asser says he could not at that time gratify his most ardent wish to learn liberal art, because, as Alfred told him, there were then no good readers in all the kingdom of the West Saxons.[1] Indeed, he confessed to Asser with many lamentations and inmost sighs of his heart that the greatest of all the difficulties and impediments of his life had been that when he was young, and had the capacity for learning,

---

[1] A marginal note in the Cotton MS. remarks that this disposes of the story of a school of literature at Oxford at that time. An interpolation in Asser credits this school with the high approval of Germanus in A.D. 430.

he could not find teachers ; and when he was more advanced in life, he was so harassed by a disease unknown to all the physicians of the island, as well as by anxieties of sovereignty, internal and external, and continual invasions of pagans, that there was no time for reading, even his masters and writers being to some extent disturbed in their occupations. But yet he never to the end of his life ceased from the insatiable desire of knowledge.

Asser makes no reference to his traditional skill as a harpist and minstrel. Probably it was a matter of course. Two hundred years before, Cædmon, in Northumbria, had fled the festive society of his labouring fellows, because he alone of them, when the harp was passed to him in turn, could not sing ; and the sense of isolation in this respect wrought so strongly in his mind that in the dreams of the night he created song, and next morning he remembered the dignified and stately creation. Aldhelm was singing in Wessex in Cædmon's time, sitting on the parapet of Malmesbury bridge, and beguiling people to sacred thought by the attraction of his secular lays.[1] We have no examples still surviving of English musical notation of Alfred's time ; but many examples exist of the next century, as, for instance, the manuscript written in Wessex about eighty years after Alfred's death for Æthelwold, Bishop of

---

[1] See also note on p. 76.

Winchester, which includes the kyrie *Rex Splendens*, composed by Dunstan, who was born in 925. There can practically be little doubt that Alfred had a similar notation, consisting of very rudimentary musical notes, with guide-letters showing time and expression. It was, however, the century after his death that saw the great development of this principle in England. Up to that time the tradition of the plain-song introduced by Augustine had been handed down from ear to ear. The chief use of our musical notation was to guard against the loss or serious variation of the traditional plain-song and the more complicated additions made by Dunstan and other skilled musicians. The Wessex churchmen learned their rugged plain-song so well, that after the Norman Conquest the monks of Glastonbury suffered death at the hands of the Norman soldiers rather than abandon their insular use for the lighter graces of the plain-song of William of Fescamp.

Alfred's warfare against the Danes began before he was king. It was in his eyes much more than a warfare against violent invaders of his territory; it was to him, above all, a religious war. That the enemy were pagans, and that part of their aim was to obliterate Christianity, that was his chief stimulus. To the Danes also it was a religious war. The Angles and Saxons and Jutes, whose lands they pillaged, were their own very distant cousins;

they had in times past worshipped the same deities whom now the Danes worshipped. To the Danes they were renegades from the one religion which the Danes held for truth. Asser knew well the king's feeling on this subject. He describes at some length the series of battles which brought Alfred into prominence, and he describes them from information received from Alfred. He never describes the combatants as English and Danes; he always speaks of them as Christians and pagans.

The first instance we have of the bent of Alfred's mind after he came to maturity occurs in connection with this feeling on his part that to fight the Danes was a religious work. In 871, just before he came to the throne, the pagan army fought against the Earl of Berkshire at Englefield, and the Christians gained the victory. Four days later, Alfred and his brother King Ethelred attacked the pagans at Reading, where they had strong fortifications. They cut to pieces such of the pagans as they found outside the fortifications; but the main body of the pagans sallied forth, and the Christians fled. Four days after, the pagan army was on strong ground at Æscesdun, the hill of the ash, and the Christians, in shame and indignation, roused by the calamity at Reading, determined to attack them under Ethelred and Alfred.

Ethelred was a religious man, as Alfred was, but his religion took practically a different form.

The king prepared for the fight by hearing mass, and the army waited for him. The pagans did not wait. Time pressed. Alfred, who was second in command, became very anxious. The king, who commanded the force arrayed against the pagan king, was still set in prayer. He declared he would not depart, alive, till the priest had done, nor leave the divine service. Alfred was to deal with the two pagan jarls ; he must either retreat or charge without waiting for his brother. Relying on the divine counsels he charged, and after a long and severe fight, in which many of the leading pagans were killed, the Christians won the day. They strewed the whole plain of Æscesdun with pagans, slaughtered in their flight. Alfred himself, it should be observed, was from childhood a frequent visitor of holy places, for the sake of prayer and almsgiving. It was certainly not from any disregard of prayer or of God's house and the public worship of God that he fought while Ethelred heard mass.

That same year, after another great fight at Basing in which the pagans got the victory, Alfred became king on the death of his brother ; Ethelred's son Ethelwold being too young to reign. A month later the pagans defeated him at Wilton. Eight pitched battles in one year, besides endless skirmishes by night and day in which Alfred and his chief men were engaged without rest or cessation against the pagans : that is Asser's summary of the year which saw Alfred mount the throne of the West Saxons.

The same note of a religious war is struck in the campaign in which Alfred finally triumphed. He issued forth from his stronghold in the marsh of Athelney to make frequent assaults upon the pagans. In the seventh week after Easter, 878, he rode to Ecgbryht's Stone (Brixton-Deverill) in the eastern part of the Selwood, or Great Wood, in British Coit Mawr, and on the third day reached Edington, where he fought with valour and persistence against the pagans and defeated them completely, killing all who were not within the earthworks. The survivors he hemmed in for fourteen days. At the end of that time the pagans were worn out, and begged for terms of peace. Their leader Guthrum proposed to become a Christian. It was agreed that those who would be baptized might settle in England ; those who would remain pagan must leave the island.[1] In the final terms, as in every phrase of Asser's story, it stands out as a religious war, and as a great religious victory it ended. From that time Christian Danes and Christian Saxons could agree.

[1] In the form of treaty as it has come down to us, there is no mention of Christianity, except so far as this, that it is confirmed by an oath for themselves and their " successors born and unborn who love God's mercy and ours." The tradition probably mixes up the simple terms of peace with the events that followed, and treats those events as the fulfilment of conditions.

II

HIS REIGN

His early years as king—Communications with Rome—
Education of his children and others—His own labours
—Religious exercises—Introduction of learned men—
Invention of candle-clocks—Distribution of income—
Foundation of monasteries—Formation of his Manual—
Embassies to foreign parts—Ecclesiastical laws.

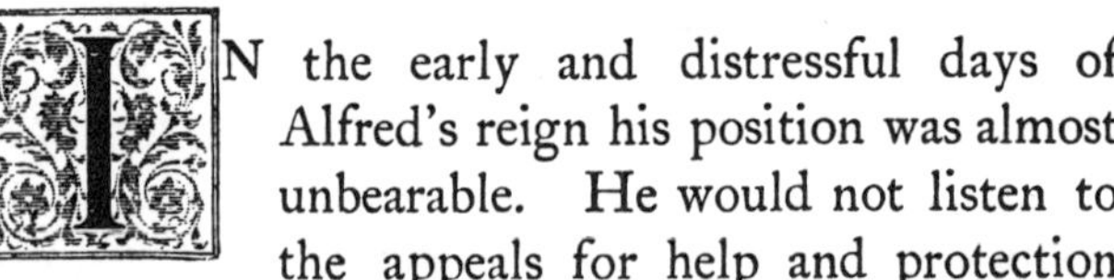IN the early and distressful days of
Alfred's reign his position was almost
unbearable. He would not listen to
the appeals for help and protection
pressed upon him by his subjects. What was
there that he could do to help and protect them ?
He was maturing his plans ; meanwhile, he repulsed his subjects, and paid, or seemed to pay, no
heed to their requests. The holy man St. Neot,
who was his relation — some say his father's
brother—often told him that he would suffer great
adversity on this account, but Alfred turned, or
seemed to turn, a deaf ear to the reproofs of the

man of God. His sin, Asser tells us, did not go unpunished; Alfred fell into so great misery that sometimes none of his subjects knew where he was or what had become of him. If this is true, it is sufficiently accounted for by his grave anxieties, and the terrible and mysterious disease which seized him suddenly in the midst of his marriage feast in 868, three years before his accession, and never left him free from pain, or the threat of pain, from the twentieth to the forty-fourth year of his age. But most probably the episode is merely part of the legendary life of St. Neot, inserted after Asser's time in his *Life of Alfred*.

Among other cares of the first ten or eleven years of his reign, he turned his attention to the English school in Rome, and persuaded Pope Martin to free it from tribute and tax. This is the Pope who absolved Bishop Formosus from his excommunication by Pope John VIII. and from his vow not to return to Rome; a reversal which led to the trial and condemnation of the dead body of Formosus, mentioned on a later page.

Alfred was now free to devote himself to the restoration of religion and learning. His own family management was a pattern to all. His youngest son, Ethelwerd, was sent to the schools which Alfred had by that time established. Here

he was taught in company with the children of
almost all the nobility of the kingdom, and many
that were not noble. They learned to read both
Latin and Saxon books, and they learned to write ;
so that by the time they were ready to practise
the manly arts—hunting and such pursuits as be-
fitted noblemen—they had become studious and
clever in the liberal arts. His older children
had been taught at home, and no less carefully. They learned the Psalms and read Saxon
books, especially Saxon poems ; at the time
when Asser wrote, Edward and Ethelswith [1]
were continually in the habit of making use of
books.

The king himself led a laborious life. Invasions by pagans, and his constantly recurring and
disabling bodily pain, did not prevent his carrying
on the government with vigour. And he was full
of other occupations. Hunting in all its branches
he continued to practise. He taught his workers
of gold,[2] one of whom no doubt had made in the

---

[1] Nothing is said of her training in needlework. The skill of the Saxon
ladies was great. There is contemporary evidence of this in the tapestry-
work figures of the stole of Frithestan, now in the Chapter Library at
Durham, worked under the direction of Alfred's daughter-in-law Ælflæd,
between 910 and 915. A Latin inscription states that *Ælflæd ordered it to be
made for the pious Bishop Frithestan.* The most gorgeous cope seen by Anselm
at the Council of Bari in 1098 had been a Canterbury vestment in Canute's
time.

[2] Frithestan's stole is a wonderful example of weaving in gold-wire, beaten
flat like narrow tape. It is woven with selvedged openings for the insertion
of the prophets, etc., these figures being made in tapestry-work.

earlier years of his reign the ornament of gold and enamel found at Athelney in 1693 and now in the Bodleian, with its legend speaking of his personal care, *Alfred had me made.* He trained artificers of all kinds ; he trained his falconers, hawkers, and kennel-men. By his own mechanical inventions he was able to build houses beyond all precedent of his ancestors. He learned by heart the Saxon poems and made others learn them ; he recited Saxon books ; he alone never desisted from studying most diligently to the best of his ability. He attended mass and the other daily religious services ; he was frequent in singing psalms and in prayer, at the day hours and the night hours ; he went to the churches at night to pray secretly, unknown to his courtiers. He was in the habit of hearing the Divine Scriptures read by his own countrymen, or, if it so happened, in the company of foreigners. His bishops, too, and all ecclesiastics, his earls and nobles, his officers and friends, were loved by him with wonderful affection ; their sons who were bred up in the royal household were as dear to him as his own ; he had them instructed in all good morals, and never ceased to teach them letters day and night. And yet he complained to God, and to all who were admitted to intimacy with him, that the Almighty had made him ignorant of divine wisdom and of the liberal arts. He was affable and pleasant to all—that, we may depend upon it, was the truth, and not that other story of morose repulse of all who sought him—and he was curiously eager to investigate things unknown.

Determined to advance learning in his kingdom of Wessex, he invited out of Mercia four very learned men of that nation.   They were Werefrith, Bishop of Worcester, who translated the dialogues of Gregory and Peter into Saxon; Plegmund, afterwards Archbishop of Canterbury, the founder of the Saxon Chronicle; and the priests Ethelstan and Werewulf.   Night and day, whenever there was leisure, one of these four read to him; so that he possessed a knowledge of every book, though as yet he could not himself read his books.

Further, he sent to Gaul for teachers, and two especially are named.   These were Grimbald, the provost of St. Omer, a good singer, prominent in ecclesiastical discipline and good morals, very learned in Holy Scripture, and John of Corbey, learned in all kinds of literature and skilled in many arts.   Asser, who was of the greatest service to him, he persuaded to come to him out of South Wales; Asser's own account of the bargaining is very quaint.   Asser's principal function was, as we have seen in the case of the four Mercians, to read to him night and day whenever there was time.   Alfred carried his determination to have learned men in important places so far that he would rather keep a bishopric vacant than fill it with an unlearned man. That he had the income of vacant bishoprics has been made a charge against him. An examination of the dates of death of bishops in Alfred's dominions and the dates of consecration of their successors fails to provide any serious ground for a charge of this kind.

The story of Alfred's invention of candles to measure the time is well known. It is not so well known that his desire to measure time correctly came from a religious motive. His determination was to give to God half his time, day and night. So far as the day was concerned, if the sun was visible the division could be made ; but clouds by day baffled him, and at night there was darkness. Hence the invention of the candles, which were measured to burn four hours each. Each candle was divided into twelve equal parts by lines on the surface. The invention of a lantern followed, for a reason which sets before us the discomforts of life in those times. The candles did not burn steadily and evenly, for the flame was blown about by the violence of the wind, which blew day and night without intermission through the doors and windows of the churches, the fissures of the divisions, the plankings, the walls, or the sides of the tents. Alfred made boxes for the lights, with doors of white ox-horn planed so thin that they were like glass. There are small niches in some of our churches now, with signs of doors, probably for protecting the lights at night from the draught.

And as he gave half of his time to God, so he gave half of his income. Ethelwulf, his father, had released from tribute to the king one-tenth part of the royal estates,[1] for the glory of God and his own eternal salvation. Alfred divided his income into two equal parts, for secular and for ecclesiastical expenditure. The secular half was divided into three equal parts. The first was for his soldiers and the nobles who attended at his court and performed divers functions ; these latter were in three sets, each of which performed one month's service in each quarter and spent two months at home. The next third went to the operatives whom he had collected from every nation, of great skill in every kind of construction ; workers in gold are specially mentioned in another part of Asser's description. The remaining third went to foreigners who visited him, whether they asked for money or not. So much for the secular half of his income.

The second half of each year's income was all given to God. It was divided into four parts. The first part was for the poor of all

[1] This is variously stated.

nations.[1]   It was to be discreetly bestowed ; for the king said that, as far as could be, Pope Gregory's saying should be fulfilled, give not much to whom you should give little, nor little to whom much, nor something to whom nothing, nor nothing to whom something.   The second was for the two monasteries which Alfred had specially founded, at Athelney and Shaftesbury.   The third went to his school, which he had studiously collected together, of many of the nobility of his own kingdom.   The fourth was for all the neighbouring monasteries in all Saxony and Mercia, and in some years for monasteries in Wales, Cornwall, Gaul, Brittany, Northumbria, and sometimes Ireland.   It is a remarkable fact that in this large expenditure for religious purposes, the purposes are at most only indirectly connected with the definitely spiritual work of ministering the Word of God and the Sacraments to the people at large.

Asser is not very clear in the sequence of his ideas.   But we gather that the king's desire to found monasteries was due to his own fixed purpose of holy meditation, to which he desired to invite others.   But he could not find any one of his own nation, free by birth, who was willing to adopt the monastic life, except some who were

---

[1] Here as elsewhere we may suppose that the various races in these islands are meant.   The list of countries given under the fourth head is probably a sufficient guide to the meaning of the phrase.

mere children, too young to choose between good and evil. The love of the monastic life, once so strong in England, had died out. Asser theorises as to the reasons for this, and he produces two which seem to be mutually destructive : it was either because of the constant invasions by sea and land, or because people abounded in riches of every kind and so despised the monastic life. He had to get an old Saxon to act as Abbot of his new foundation of Athelney ; and then some priests and deacons from across the seas ; and then, as he had not nearly plenty of inmates, he got as many Gauls as he possibly could, including children, to be reared to the monastic life. Asser had himself seen a lad of pagan birth who was educated there, and who was by no means the hindmost of them all.

The formation of King Alfred's Manual, which is not known to exist, may best be told something as Asser tells it. He says that it was in 887 or 888 that the king first formed the desire to interpret passages of Scripture to those who did not know Latin.

" We were talking together one day, and I read to him an extract from a certain book. He heard it with both his ears. He brought out his book with the daily courses and psalms and the prayers he had read in his youth, and commanded me to write there the quotation. I turned it over, and found it very nearly full. After some delay I said, had I not better find another sheet on which this might be entered apart ; for perhaps some other quotation might occur, and if so we should be glad to have them kept together ? 'Your plan is good,' he said. So I made haste and got a sheet and wrote the quotation. That same day no less than three other passages pleased him ; and from that time we talked daily and wrote such things as pleased him till at last it was full, for he went on unceasingly collecting many flowers of Divine Scriptures. When the first quotation was copied onto the sheet, he at once became anxious to read and interpret it in Saxon, and to teach others. The book grew till it became almost as large as a Psalter. He called it his Manual, because he kept it carefully at hand day and night, and found, as he told me, no small consolation therein."

It was not to Rome only that Alfred sent messengers and gifts. Asser speaks, with Celtic breadth, of daily embassies sent to foreign nations, from the Tyrrhenian sea to the farthest end of Ireland.[1] The English Chronicle goes further. Alfred vowed, it is said, when they were set against

---

[1] A mediæval editor proposes to read Hiberiæ instead of Hiberniæ, Spain instead of Ireland. But the English Chronicle tells of a visit to Alfred in 891 of three Scots, that is, Irishmen, smitten with the desire to wander. A later Chronicle assigns their departure from their own land to the death of their favourite teacher Swifneh. He was known as the most wise, or most skilled, of the Scots, and the English Chronicle mentions his death. His

the enemy in London, to send embassies to St. Thomas and St. Bartholomew. The Chronicle, under the year 883, tells us that he sent gifts to India. William of Malmesbury informs us that Sigelm, Bishop of Sherborne, was sent as ambassador with the gifts to St. Thomas, and that he prosperously penetrated into India. Thus, Dean Hook remarks, the first intercourse between England and Hindustan consisted of this interchange of Christian feeling. It is, however, a little curious that Asser never mentions India, nor did Alfred interpolate any mention of his embassy when translating Orosius for his English people. Asser definitely mentions Judea, telling us that he had seen letters to Alfred which came with presents from Abel the Patriarch of Jerusalem. It may be worth mention that other MSS. of the English Chronicle read Iudia and Iudea instead of India. Still, the fact of the journey of Alfred's messengers to some distant part which then bore the name of India, seems to be accepted on all hands. There is no very violent improbability about it. Christian missionaries from Persia had reached India and China more than three centuries before this, two of them bringing the silk-worm to the Greek empire in Justinian's reign, about 550. The

beautiful Celtic grave slab is at Clonmacnoise. The close connection which existed between the early Anglo-Saxons and the Irish schools of learning had now ceased.

Egyptian merchant - monk Cosmas wrote his *Christian Topography* at that date. He found Nestorian Christians in Ceylon and Malabar, but the king and people of Ceylon were still heathens.

Alfred's Ecclesiastical Laws have a long preface, apparently prepared by himself. It is an interesting piece of argument. First he gives the Ten Commandments in Saxon. Writers inform us that he omits the Second Commandment, in accordance with the evil practice which had already made considerable progress then ; but probably these writers did not read to the end, for Alfred's Tenth Commandment is, " Thou shalt not make to thyself golden gods nor silvern." Then he points out that our Saviour, Christ, said He came not to break nor forbid these Commandments, but with all good to increase them, and mercy and humility He taught. Then he quotes the decisions of the church at Jerusalem as to the tenderness of the application of the law to the Gentile converts. When the English race became Christian, he proceeds, they held synods of holy bishops and great and wise men. They then ordained, out of that mercy which Christ had taught, that secular lords, by the synod's leave, might without sin take for almost every misdeed, for the first offence, the money fine ordained by the synod. They then in many synods ordained a fine for many human misdeeds, and in many synod-books they wrote, at one place one doom, at another another.

The one offence to which they dared not assign any mercy, that is, any bot, or money fine, was treason to a lord ; because God Almighty adjudged no mercy to those who despised Him, nor did Christ, the Son of God, adjudge any to him who sold Him to death, and He commanded that a lord should be loved as Himself.

This is a very interesting explanation of the Saxon system of money payments for offences of almost every description. It is not altogether unlike in principle to the modern magistrate-law that a dog has his first bite free. That application of the principle found no favour with King Alfred, in whose days dogs were great and dangerous beasts. If a dog tear or bite a man, for the first misdeed, 6s. ; for the second, 12s. ; for the third, 30s. If the dog do more misdeeds, the owner is to go on paying, or must repudiate the dog.

" These many dooms I, Alfred the king, gathered together ; and commanded many to be written of those our forefathers held which to me seemed good ; and many of those which seemed to me not good, I rejected them by the counsel of my wise men. I durst not venture to set down much of my own, for it was unknown to me what of it would please those who should come after us."

Three characteristic dooms may be quoted,

"He who steals on Sunday, or at Christmas or Easter, or on Holy Thursday,[1] or on Rogation days,[2] or during Lent, shall pay a twofold bot." "If a man go to the church, and reveal an offence not revealed, and confess himself in God's name, be it half forgiven."   For holidays,—" To all freemen, 12 days at Yule, and the day on which Christ overcame the devil, and the commemoration day of St. Gregory, and 7 days before Easter and 7 after, and one day at St. Peter's tide, and one day at St. Paul's tide, and in harvest the whole week before St. Mary-mass, and one day at the celebration of All Hallows, and the 4 Wednesdays in Ember weeks,"—forty-two days in all, making, with the addition of Sundays, just a quarter of the whole year.

[1] We have lost the sense of paganism in the names of our days, but it comes out quaintly in the Saxon form, *on thone Halgan Thunres dæg*.

[2] Still called in Yorkshire, as in Alfred's Ecclesiastical Law, gang-days.

III

His translations—Bede's *Ecclesiastical History of the English
Race*—*The Pastoral Care*—State of learning in Wessex,
Mercia, and Northumbria—Ideal of a bishop's life—
Orosius—Boethius—Alfred's religious opinions—John
the Scot—Alfred's will—Hyde Abbey—State of Rome
—Religious references—Religious bequests—Slaves.

HE general drift of Alfred's opinion as
to the sort of learning most needed
by his people is to be gathered from
his choice of books to be put before
them in their native language.   These were four.
For general history, and for history and geography
relating to their own race on the continent of
Europe, he chose Orosius : for mental study, the
Consolation of Boethius : for realisation of the
true principles of the life and work of religion,
the *Pastoral Care :* for the Church history of
the English people, of course the great and priceless book of the Venerable Bede.   Of this last we
need say nothing.   Nor need we dwell upon the

fact that Alfred may be said to have created the continuity of early English history by his establishment of the Anglo-Saxon Chronicle under Plegmund.

The preface to Alfred's translation into English from the Latin of Pope Gregory's *Pastoral Care*, a treatise on the life and work of a bishop, gives us so clear an insight into the king's mind, and such valuable information as to the state of learning in his time, that it deserves to be printed in full. Three of the copies of which the king speaks are in existence, one addressed to Archbishop Plegmund of Canterbury, one to Bishop Wulfsige of Sherborne, and the third to Bishop Werefrith of Worcester.

This Book is for Worcester

King Alfred greets Bishop Wærferth with loving words and with friendship. I let it be known to thee that it has very often come into my mind, what wise men there formerly were throughout England, both of sacred and secular orders ; and how happy times there were then throughout England ; and how the kings who had power over the nation in those days obeyed God and his ministers ; and they preserved peace, morality, and order at home, and at the same time enlarged their territory abroad ; and how they prospered both with war and with wisdom ; and also the sacred orders how zealous they were both in teaching and learning, and in all the services they owed to God ; and how foreigners came to this land in search of wisdom and instruction, and how we should now have to get teachers from abroad if we were to have them. So general was the decay in England that there were very few on this side of the Humber who could understand their rituals in English, or translate a letter from Latin into English; and I believe that there were not many beyond the Humber. There were so few of them that I cannot remember a single one south of the Thames when I came to the throne. Thanks be to God Almighty that we have any teachers among us now. And therefore I command thee to do as I believe thou art willing, to disengage thyself from worldly matters as often as may be, that thou mayest apply the wisdom which God has given thee wherever thou canst.[1] Consider what punishments would come upon us on account of this world, if we neither loved wisdom ourselves nor suffered other men to obtain it: we should love the name only of Christian, and very few of the virtues. When I considered all this I remembered also how I saw in my own early days, before all had been ravaged and burnt, how the churches throughout the whole of England stood filled with treasures and books, and there was also a great multitude of God's servants. But they had very little knowledge of the books, for they could not understand anything of them because they were not written in their own language. As if they had said: " Our forefathers, who formerly held these places, loved wisdom, and through it they obtained wealth and bequeathed it to us. In this we can still see their tracks, but we cannot follow them,

---

[1] Even of the famous scholar Aldhelm, 200 years before, it was said that when he became bishop he was absorbed, as the manner of bishops was, in the secular cares of his position.

and therefore we have lost both the wealth and the wisdom, because we would not incline our hearts after their example." When I remembered all this, I wondered extremely that the good and wise men who were formerly all over England, and had perfectly learnt all the books, did not wish to translate them into their own language. But again I soon answered myself and said : They did not think that men would ever be so careless, and that learning would thus decay ; so they abstained from translating, and they hoped that wisdom in this land would increase, and our knowledge of languages. Then I remembered how the law was first known in Hebrew, and again, when the Greeks had learnt it, they translated the whole of it into their own language, and all other books besides. And again, the Romans, when they had learnt it, they translated the whole of it through learned interpreters into their own language. And also all other Christian nations translated parts of it into their own languages. Therefore it seems better to me, if ye think so, for us also to translate some books which are most needful for all men to know into the language which we can all understand. And I would have you do as we very easily can if we have tranquillity enough, that is, set all the youth now in England of free men, who are rich enough to be able to devote themselves to it, to learn, as long as they are not old enough for other occupations, until they are well able to read English writing. And let those be afterwards taught more in the Latin language who are to continue learning and be promoted to a higher rank. When I remembered how the knowledge of Latin had formerly decayed throughout England, and yet many could read English writing, I began, among other various and manifold troubles of this kingdom, to translate into

English the book which is called in Latin *Pastoralis*, and in English *Shepherd's Book*, sometimes word for word and sometimes according to the sense, as I had learnt it from Plegmund my archbishop, and Asser my bishop, and Grimbold my mass-priest, and John my mass-priest.[1] And when I had learnt it as I could best understand it and as I could most clearly interpret it, I translated it into English ; and I will send a copy to every bishopric in my kingdom ; and on each there is a [clasp and chain][2] worth fifty mancuses. And I command in God's name that no man take the [clasp] from the book or the book from the minster. It is uncertain how long there may be such learned bishops as, thanks be to God, there now are nearly everywhere ; therefore I wish these books always to remain in their place, unless the bishop wish to take them with him, or they be lent out anywhere, or any one make a copy from them.

Then the book itself is made to speak, as the Cross speaks in the early Anglian Dream of the Holy Rood :—

This message Augustine over the salt sea brought from the south to the islanders, as the Lord's champion had formerly indited it, the Pope of Rome. The wise Gregorius was versed in many true doctrines through the wisdom of his mind, his hoard of studious thoughts. For he gained over most of mankind to the Guardian of

---

[1] His translation of this book is much closer to the original than is the case with his History (Bede), Geography (Orosius), and Philosophy (Boethius).

[2] Perhaps a desk and pointer. See Professor Earle's remarks in this volume.

April

May

June

THE SEASONS—APRIL TO JUNE

heaven, best of Romans, wisest of men, most gloriously famous. Afterwards King Alfred brought every word of me into English, and sent me to his scribes south and north ; ordered more such to be brought to him, that he might send them to his bishops, for some of them needed it, who knew but little Latin.

It is not our business here to consider the contents of Pope Gregory's treatise on the shepherding of the people. But the headings of two or three of the sixty-five chapters will show what the attraction for Alfred's mind was. The first chapter argues " that unlearned men are not to presume to undertake teaching." To prevent this was a purpose with Alfred ; he faced obloquy, it is said, rather than fill bishoprics with unlearned men. The second chapter forbids even learned men to undertake to teach if they are not ready to live in accordance with their own precepts. The third and fourth chapters no doubt appealed to himself as a secular governor, though they related to spiritual government, " how he who governs must despise all hardships, and how afraid he must be of every luxury," and " how often the occupations of power and government distract the mind of the ruler." The sixty-fifth chapter brings the whole to a conclusion with an argument thoroughly after Alfred's own heart : " When any one has performed all the duties of his pastoral charge, let him then consider and understand his own self, lest either his exemplary life or his successful teaching puff him up."

In his translation of the history and geography of Orosius he does not interpolate information where we might not unnaturally have expected him to do so. Of his large and valuable interpolations of a geographical character, and in regard to the history of the Teutonic races, mention is no doubt made in another chapter. In the sixth book, to mention two cases where Orosius writes of the times of Constantius and Constantine, and makes references to Britain, he does not speak of Christianity here, and Alfred does not add anything. Orosius speaks of many martyrs under Diocletian, not localising any. Again, Alfred does not add anything. Two quaint phrases the king employs :—" In those days Arius the mass-priest was in error with regard to the right faith ";— " Constantine was the first emperor who ordered churches to be built, and locked up the devil's houses."

It is not to be wondered at that Alfred determined to translate into English the *Consolation* of Boethius, and his interpolations show how dear the book was to his heart and to his reason. King and people alike had gone through much trial and suffering, and such happiness and prosperity as they had was at best very precarious. The book of *Consolation* which Boethius wrote in the sad days when all his great prosperity had passed from him, and he waited in chains for the last fatal word of the tyrant, was well suited for men and women situated as the English then were. Boethius himself, who was executed in 524, was both a very learned Christian and a deeply-read student of classical philosophy. His Consolations are taken entirely from philosophy, but they have the Christian spirit. They thus supplement the help which the Christian religion gives to those in anxiety, and put into the troubled mind fresh and useful trains of thought. This is probably one main reason for the attraction which the book had in the Middle Ages, and we cannot doubt that Alfred had this in view in giving it to his people. Why he did not at the same time have the New Testament translated into English is not clear, for he himself pointed out, in his Preface to the *Pastoral Care*, that the law was first given in Hebrew, and then necessarily translated into Greek, and Latin, and the languages of the various nations which embraced Christianity. William of Malmesbury tells us that the king did as a matter of fact set about translating the Psalter, but died before the first part was done.

Besides the hint which his translation of Boethius gives, it is on another account probable that Alfred took a broad view of religious questions. If the evidence is to be accepted as sufficient, he was a patron of Johannes Scotus Erigena. John the Scot, that is, as we should now say, the Irishman, had made the Continent too hot to hold him by the breadth of his religious views. He refused to distinguish religion from philosophy, an attitude of mind which may have specially influenced Alfred, who had probably known him as a boy at the court of Charles the Bald, where John acted as tutor to Judith. He had maintained, too, that authority, when it is not confirmed by reason, is of no value. He had made a determined stand against the new and materialistic teaching on the Real Presence, known as transubstantiation. He found a refuge at the court of Alfred. This can scarcely have meant less than that Alfred, to some extent at least, shared his opinions ; and if that was so, we see an additional reason for Alfred's admiration of Boethius, and we have some explanation of the character of the provisions of the will by which the king disposed of his property.

In those days, and in days earlier still, to teach an unpopular opinion was a dangerous thing. Great violence was not unknown in schools of learning. Even in modern times we hear a good deal of the violence of students in Paris and in other universities of the Continent. When Archbishop Theodore came over to England in 664 and began to teach, there were very sharp passages at arms between the teacher and the Irish students who attended his lectures. Aldhelm was a student at Canterbury at the time, and he describes one of these encounters, where the Irish students baited their lecturer, Archbishop though he was. The old student and lecturer of the University of Athens was more than a match for them. "He treated them," Aldhelm wrote to a friend, "as the truculent boar treats the Molossian hounds. He tore them with the tusk of grammar, and shot them with the deep and sharp syllogisms of chronography, till they cast away their weapons and hurriedly fled to the recesses of their dens." In Wessex the students went further still. One John—almost certainly not the famous John of whom we are speaking, though mediæval writers took him to be the same—so irritated the students of the great school of Malmesbury, that they set on him with the sharp iron styles of the time, which represented our modern pens, and inflicted wounds of which he died. William of Malmesbury gives the epitaph of this John from a tomb on the left side of the altar at Malmesbury ; he is described as the holy sophist John, and is said to have been a martyr. William does not absolutely identify him with Johannes Erigena, but he describes him as Johannes Scottus, and says that he had been at the court of Charles the Bald, and was attracted by the munificence of Alfred. We may fairly say that William believed their John to be the Erigena, and we may almost certainly say that in that belief he was wrong.

John the Erin-born is usually said to have died about 886. There is thus no difficulty on the score of dates in the way of his being at Alfred's court. He must have been an oldish man, for he was a prominent controversialist as early as 854.

Alfred's will is on all accounts a document of very great interest. We have noticed already the provisions of his father's will, so far as they have been preserved for us, and with these we cannot but contrast the corresponding parts of Alfred's disposition of his property. Many details of the will we must for our present purpose pass by, notwithstanding their general importance : they are no doubt dealt with in another chapter.

Alfred's will exists in an Anglo-Saxon form and in a Latin form. It is preserved in the Register of Newminster, which Alfred founded at Winchester. This institution was afterwards moved to Hyde. The will was copied into the Register now known as the Register of Hyde Abbey, about the years 1028-1032.

Ethelwulf had bequeathed considerable sums to the Church of St. Peter and the Church of St. Paul at Rome, and to the Pope. Alfred had sent presents to Rome. From 883 to 890 there are four records of West Saxon gifts. But after 890 there is no record, and in Alfred's will no mention is made of the chief city of the Western world or of the spiritual head of the Church of the West. One explanation may be that at his death the sad period had already begun which makes men of all Christian creeds hang their heads with shame that such things could be. King Alfred's court was unique among secular courts in its purity and order ; the papal court had entered upon one of those phases in its existence where it has stood out prominently among the most impure and disorderly spots on the face of the known earth. It is enough, for any one who knows the meaning of the references, to glance at the table of contents of a Church history for the years 896 and 897 :—" Death of Pope Formosus ; Pope Boniface VII. ; trial and condemnation of the body of Formosus by Pope Stephen VI. ; Pope Stephen strangled ; Pope Romanus ; Pope Theodorus II. ; Pope John IX. ; Pope Sergius IV. ; Marquisate of Tusculum ; Theodora and Marozia." We can well understand that not all Alfred's reverence for the place where lay the bodies of St. Peter and St. Paul could overcome the effect of a record so grievous as that.

Turning to those parts of Alfred's will which have a directly religious bearing, it is impossible not to be struck by the obliqueness of the religious references. Of his reliance on divine help and his trust in divine assistance there is no doubt. He clearly regarded these as powers actually at work in the world, and as the one only means by which the actions of those who should follow him might be rightly guided. It is by God's support that he trusts his will may be carried out. He is king by God's grace. He has considered of his soul's health, and of the inheritance which God and his ancestors did give; but he is reserved and allusive where other men of the time were detailed and definite. The air of reserve would almost seem to indicate that the teaching of John the Erin-born, while it had not in the least shaken the confidence of his faith and trust, had seriously indisposed him to speak in confident detail of the relations of man's service to God's help. "Let them distribute, for me and for my father and for the friends that he interceded for and I intercede for, 200 pounds; 50 to the mass-priests all over my kingdom, 50 to the poor servants of God, 50 to the distressed poor, 50 to the church where I shall rest." "And I will that they do restore to the families at Domersham their land-deeds and their liberty to choose any man they will [*i.e.* to continue to live under that lord or to choose another], for me and for Ælflæd [his eldest daughter] and for the friends that she did intercede for and I do intercede for." "And let them also seek with a living price[1] for

---

[1] The words in the Saxon will are *sec man eac on cwicum ceape*; in the Latin will, *imploretur deus viventi pretio.*

my soul's health so far as may be[1] and as is fitting and as ye to give me shall be disposed." It has been clearly shown that *on cwicum ceape* was a recognised phrase for "with live stock." The reserve of Alfred's language in this, the most important part of his will in mediæval opinion, is worthy of note. Indeed, the absence of definite words which might have been expected is so marked that in another Latin copy, a very incorrect translation of part of the Anglo-Saxon will, they are added, but curiously enough are connected solely with the restoration of the land-books to the people at Domersham. The freeing of slaves was a religious work. It will be seen that as a religious work Alfred himself regarded it. "I beseech in God's name and in the name of His Saints that no one of my relations or heirs obstruct the freedom of those whom I have redeemed. The West-Saxon Witan have pronounced it lawful that I may leave them free or bond as I will. But I, for God's love and for my soul's advantage, will that they be master of their freedom and of their will; and in the name of the living God I bid that none disturb them, neither by money exaction nor by any manner of means."

It is a well-known fact that the Church set before men the duty of giving slaves their freedom.

---

[1] Saxon, *swa hit beon mæge*; Latin, *quantum fieri possit.*

Late in the seventh century, Bishop Wilfrith released 250 men and women whom he found attached as slaves to his estate of Selsey ; and Archbishop Theodore denied Christian burial to the kidnapper, and prohibited the sale of children by their parents after the age of seven. In the year 816, the archbishop and bishops of the southern province, thirteen in number, met in council at Celchyth (Chelsea), and bound themselves by canon to free at their death every Englishman, who, during their tenure of the lands of the bishoprics, had become a slave, the usual causes of enslavement in time of peace being poverty or crime. There is a canon of that council, directed against the abstraction of monastic charters and lists of landed property, which has a very modern sound about its title, "that monasteries be not deprived of their telligraphs."

We cannot close this chapter better than with Alfred's own right royal words. "I can assert this in all truth, that during the whole course of my existence I have always striven to live in a becoming manner, and at my death to leave to those who follow me a worthy memorial in my works."

ALFRED AS WARRIOR

By Charles Oman

ALFRED AS WARRIOR

OF all the aspects of Alfred's many-sided life there is none more interesting, yet more baffling, than his military career. We know its outlines : his lot fell in the direst time of storm and stress that had ever come upon the English ; he weathered the tempest which had so sorely buffeted his father and his brothers, and steered the ship of the state into calmer waters. We have a not inconsiderable bulk of records concerning his campaigns, yet again and again the why and the wherefore of triumph and defeat elude us. The all-important details which would explain why things went ill in 872 and well in 878, why Basing saw a disaster and Buttington a victory, are withheld. The unwearied king marches east and marches west, now with a large army, now with a mere handful of men ; he reaches his foes and brings them to bay ; then " the heathen are put to flight," or, on the other hand, " after great slaughter on both sides the Danes hold possession of the place of battle " ;

but whether superior tactics, or superior numbers, or superior endurance won the day is concealed from us. It is seldom that even the most vague and general features of the fight are narrated: of really important engagements like Ashdown or Eddington, or the struggle on the Lea, we know only just enough to make us desire to know more.

Fortunately we are able to make out a good deal more about the strategy than about the tactics of Alfred's campaigns. His itineraries are generally preserved, and the natural features of hill and vale and marsh and wood can easily be ascertained. Similarly there is a certain amount to be recovered concerning his work as a military organiser, though here our authorities give us hints rather than facts, and make it very hard to disentangle his reforms from those of his worthy successor, Edward the Elder.

When Alfred first looked upon the face of war, the English had been already engaged for some seventy years in their great struggle to drive off the Vikings, and were prospering little in the attempt. The period during which the invaders had contented themselves with sporadic descents on the towns and monasteries hard by the sea, was long over. They were now cutting their way deep into England from every side, and prolonging their stay more and more every year. While Alfred was still a child by his mother's knee, a yet more threatening stage had been reached : instead of returning to their homes by the Danish and Norwegian fiords, when autumn drew to an end, the enemy had begun to fortify some ness or island by the English shore, and to abide there all the winter months. The period of objectless plunder was drawing near its end, and that of settlement and conquest was approaching.

It is not hard to make out the main causes of the ineffectiveness of the resistance which the English kingdoms offered to the invader ; they were much the same as those which were to be seen in the Frankish empire on the other side of the British Channel—the want of any central organisation for combined defence—the want of any large bodies of professional fighting-men, fully equipped with the best arms of the day—the scarcity of fortified places—the non-existence of a war-fleet. In respect of the first of these matters the English were in some ways more unfortunate, in others happier, than the Franks. On the Continent the Vikings were confronted by a vast empire which was beginning to drop to pieces from its own weight ; the realm of Charlemagne would have split up into national kingdoms even if there had been no invaders from outside to hasten the process. Particularism and heritage-partition were the order of the day · it was impossible to

hope that the numerous descendants of the great
Carling house would loyally aid each other against
the external enemy, or that their heterogeneous
subjects would care much for the woes of their
neighbours.   In England, on the other hand,
the national evolution of the times was tending
towards union.   Even before the effects of the
Danish invasions began to be felt, the states of the
Heptarchy were already beginning to draw together
into larger units.   Offa the Mercian (755-794)
had been suzerain of all England in a far truer
sense than any of the early " Bretwalda " kings
that were before him.   He had annexed kingdoms
like Kent, Essex, East Anglia, instead of merely
making their monarchs do him homage.   These
states rose again for a short space at his death;
but when Egbert won the supremacy for Wessex a
few years later, the same tendency was apparent:
that great warrior was able to incorporate the old
realms of Kent and Sussex with his ancestral
dominions, nor did they ever again free themselves
from dependence on the house of Cerdic.   It was
clear that England was tending to group itself into
no more than three or four large states : the smaller
tribal nationalities were beginning to be absorbed
in the greater.   Thus, though Egbert and his successor Ethelwulf were kings south of Thames alone,
and only enjoyed a precarious suzerainty north of
it, yet there was some hope for the future.   The

fatal disruptive tendencies visible among the Franks were not paralleled on this side of the Channel.

In the second point wherein the old Christian kingdoms were at a disadvantage when struggling with the Dane—the want of a large and well-armed body of trained fighting-men—England was probably in a worse condition than her continental neighbour. Both possessed two classes of warriors —a small body of wealthy landed vassals of the king, bound to him by special oaths of allegiance, and the general levy of the country-side, torn from the plough when necessity demanded. The former were more or less professional warriors : the English "*gesithcund* man holding land," if he neglected his lord's summons to join the host, forfeited his estate and paid a crushing fine as well : the ordinary peasant, the "ceorlish man," only suffered pecuniary punishment for the same offence. The *gesiths*, or *thegns*, as they were now beginning to be called, a wealthy, well-armoured military class, were the core of the national host. The rude masses of the half-armed country folk were a far less efficient part of the military forces of the realm. But in England the thegnhood does not appear in the ninth century to have reached nearly the same stage of relative importance as had the Frankish vassals. They would seem to have been less numerous in proportion to the size of the states, and less powerful in the realm. As a combatant body, too, they

were inferior, for the Franks had taken to fighting
on horseback, and every vassal came to the host
not only well armed, but well mounted. The
English were still fighting on foot like their ancestors : they did not, indeed, learn cavalry service
till the eleventh century. In contending with an
active and rapidly moving enemy like the Dane,
this want of horsemen was a terrible drawback to
the English host.

The third source of weakness which we have
named—the scarcity of well-fortified strongholds—
was felt both on this and on the other side of the
Channel. Neither Frank nor Anglo-Saxon had
made any systematic attempt to keep up the great
fortresses which they had inherited from the
Romans. But here again the English were at a
greater disadvantage than their continental neighbours. They had neglected scientific fortification
even more than the Franks. They mostly dwelt in
open towns and villages ; even the ancient Roman
walls of great cities like London and York had
been allowed to fall into decay. At most they
surrounded important positions with a ditch and a
stockade ; of the building of an actual wall we
hear only at one place, the Northumbrian capital
of Bamborough. The Franks, among whom city
life was far more important than in England, seem
to have done somewhat more in the way of keeping up the old Roman *enceintes* of their great

towns.   They had also taken of late to the building of strongholds destined to hold down conquered territory.   Charlemagne had warred down the obstinate Saxons mainly by rearing line after line of *burgs* among their heaths and forests.   No great English king had yet tried to maintain his control over his vassal-states by such an expedient.   Even if the Frankish *burgs* were but concentric rings of ditch, mound, and palisade, they were by no means lacking in importance in the day of danger.

In the matter of naval defence, on the other hand, there was more hope for England than for her continental neighbours.   The Saxons and Angles had always been seafarers : the Franks had never taken to the water.   Neither of the nations possessed any regular war-fleet, but in the one the national genius was favourable to its creation ; in the other it was not.   We hear, indeed, long before Alfred's day, of intermittent attempts of English kings to do something on the seas.   The most notable was the assault on Ireland which the Northumbrian Ecgfrith made in 684.   In the days of Alfred's own father, Ethelwulf, there was at least one endeavour to meet the Danes upon the water : the Anglo-Saxon Chronicle tells how the Kentish alderman Ealhere " fought in ships " at Sandwich, and took nine ships of the heathen, and put the rest to flight " (851).   It is possible that the same chief was engaged in a second naval battle two years later, for in an unsuccessful attempt which he made to turn the Vikings out of Thanet "there was much slaughter and many men *drowned* upon both sides." Thanet being then separated from the Kentish mainland by a broad estuary, it is conceivable that there was some fighting on shipboard on this occasion also.

But any small naval resources which England possessed in the second half of the ninth century seemed hopelessly inadequate to impose the least check on the Danes. The invaders came in squadrons numbered by the hundred vessels. Even after Alfred had begun to take in hand a scheme for building a regular fleet, the English ships were only counted in tens or scores. In our own days a power possessing some few vessels, and expecting invasion, would turn them to use by setting them to watch for the enemy, discover him, and give early knowledge of his approach, or to follow his course and divine his intentions. But such tactics demand vessels that can keep the sea for long spaces of time and in any weather. Neither English nor Danish galleys were suited for such work : they preferred coasting voyages, and touched the shore frequently, creeping from cape to cape and from isle to isle. The only voyage across a broad and open sea was that which was made when a Viking fleet ran straight across from the south-western cape of Norway instead of coasting along the Danish and Frisian shore. The Scandinavians were daring seamen, but their skill and ·pluck was shown rather by the way in which they felt their way along dangerous, rock-bound coasts, like those of the Hebrides or Western Ireland, than by passages across the high seas. For such crossings they waited for long spells of fine weather, in order to run the least possible risk. This was only natural, for their ships were but long, light, undecked vessels, depending mainly on their twelve or sixteen oars a side, and only using their sails when the wind set fair. To face a really serious Atlantic storm they were wholly unfitted, and even the rough weather of the Channel could be too much for them. In 877 a whole fleet of a hundred and twenty ships was wrecked near Swanage on the cliffs of the Isle of Purbeck. It was no wonder that they preferred to pick their weather, and to hug the shore, in order that they might run into the nearest haven when a tempest seemed at hand. The seamanship of the English was undoubtedly inferior to that of the Scandinavians in the ninth century, and we may guess that in handiness as well as in numbers they were wholly unable to vie with their enemies before Alfred's day.

The years 840-880 were the darkest period in the dismal century of the Viking raids. Neither in England nor on the Continent had there been found any effective way of resisting the invaders, nor any great warrior who could inspire his subject with the energy and courage that was needed to face the ever-growing evil. Kings like Ethelwulf or Charles the Bald, however good their intentions, were wholly inadequate to the task. Their warlike sons, Louis III., the victor of Saucourt, and Ethelred, the victor of Ashdown, were cut off in the prime of their years, just when they were beginning to win themselves a name. The Danes went where they would, no longer taking to their ships when the national levy came out against them, but stockading a camp and defying the owners of the soil to evict them from it. Almost always the assaults made on these strongholds ended in disastrous failures : it is hard to say whether the repulse of Charles the Bald at Givald's Foss (852), of Ethelred at Reading (871), or of Charles the Fat at Ashloh (882), was the more heart-breaking to the landsfolk. It seemed impossible to burst through the bristling line of stakes and ditch manned by the veteran axemen of the heathen bands.

The fact was that the rank and file of the Viking hosts were individually superior to the peasant-levies that strove to overwhelm them. In a Frankish or an English army only counts and aldermen, thegns and wealthy vassals, wore the steel helm and the ring-mail byrnie : the masses that followed them to the field had no more than spear and shield, possessing no defensive armour whatever. The Vikings, on the other hand, were professional fighting-men, armed not only with the " war-nets " that their own smiths could make, but with the spoils of a hundred victorious fights. It was no wonder that they could hold out against very superior numbers of the raw, half-armed militia of the English *Fyrd* and the Frankish *Ban*. In the ages when personal skill with axe and sword and trained agility of body counted for so much, one practised warrior was worth two farmers fresh from the plough. It required a vast preponderance of force, or a very skilled and fortunate leader, to enable the Christian host to inflict a really crushing defeat on the invaders.

When Alfred was a child the problem seemed growing more hopeless day by day. Even the greatest cities of Western Christendom were falling a prey to the heathen. London had been taken and sacked in 851, Tours in 853, Paris in 857, Winchester in 860. The invading hordes, now carried in fleets of three or four hundred sail, came ashore where they would, seized horses in the country-side and rode across the land, plundering far and wide, to some appointed spot to which their fleet came round and joined them. Or they would draw their ships ashore at some convenient estuary, set a guard over them, and send the rest of the host to make a circular raid, which finally took them back to their camp and their vessels. The former plan was the better, since if the ships ran out to sea after throwing ashore the landing force, the defenders of the realm did not know where the march of the enemy would be directed ; while if the fleet was immobilised on some ness or island, it was easy to intercept the raiders, who were bound to make their way back to their base.

The lowest pitch of despair seemed to be reached when in many regions rulers and people ceased to try to defend themselves against the Danes, and merely strove to procure a precarious respite from their oppressors by bribing them to depart and transfer their ravages to other shores. This was done in 865 by the Kentishmen, in 866 by the East Angles, in 869 by the Mercians. Of course the expedient was futile ; the news that one Viking host had received a handsome tribute only drew down another, set on obtaining similar booty.

Finally, there came the last step of all : not content with plunder and blackmail the invaders began to think of taking up their permanent residence in the land and making its unfortunate inhabitants their subjects. The idea had already occurred to Jarl Thorgils in Ireland, but his ephemeral kingdom had disappeared at his murder. Now it was renewed in England in 868, after the battle of York, the most fearful disaster which had yet befallen any of the Christian kingdoms. The

Danes had stormed the Northumbrian capital : they had slain the two rival kings, Osbert and Ella, who combined to attack them : all the thegnhood of the northern realm had perished. Taking up their quarters in the ancient city of Edwin and Oswald, the conquerors began to parcel out the neighbouring region among themselves as a permanent possession.

It was in the year after this terrible downfall of the Northern Kingdom that Alfred made his first campaign. He was now nineteen, and had just married his Mercian bride, Ealhswith, the daughter of Alderman Ethelred. The enterprise in which he was engaged was one of a very typical character —a dozen expeditions with the same unfortunate end could be cited from the English and Frankish annals of the third quarter of the ninth century. A large Viking host had entered Mercia and forced its way up the Trent as far as Nottingham. King Burgred sent to Wessex to beg the aid of his brother-in-law Ethelred, who marched to his help, taking his brother Alfred with him as second in command. The united hosts of the two English realms were too large for the Vikings to dare to face them in the open field. They stockaded themselves in a great camp on the banks of the Trent and waited to be attacked. The landsfolk laid siege to the stronghold, and strove to storm it ; but they utterly failed to break their way in.

After lying some time before it, they dispersed in despair : Ethelred and Alfred went home : the unfortunate Burgred then asked for terms, and got rid of the Vikings for a short space by paying them a large tribute.   The Danes returned to York, lay there for one year, and then threw themselves upon the East Angles.   They slew King Edmund, "the Martyr," scattered his army, sacked the towns and monasteries of Norfolk and Suffolk, and made themselves masters of the whole realm (870).

Next year the turn of Wessex came : the Mercians had at least bought two years of respite by the treaty of Nottingham.   Marching from East Anglia the "Grand Army" of the Vikings crossed the Thames, seized Reading, and stockaded a great camp in the angle between the Kennet and the Thames to serve as a base for their ravaging parties. But in spite of a dozen disasters suffered during the last forty years at the hands of the same enemy, the spirit of Wessex was not yet quenched.   Its shire-levies loyally answered King Ethelred's call, and gathered in great strength opposite the Danish camp. The Berkshire fyrd even succeeded in bringing to bay and destroying at Englefield a large plundering party headed by a Jarl.   But the main body of the Vikings was not so easily disposed of. A general attack on their stronghold, headed by Ethelred and Alfred, proved wholly unfortunate.

When the assailants had wearied themselves in vain attempts to hew their way through the stockade, and drew off repulsed, the enemy made a sudden sortie : "bursting out of the gates like wolves," they fell on the shattered ranks of the men of Wessex, drove them away, and held possession of the battle spot. Thinking apparently that the English were disposed of so far as further fighting was concerned, the Vikings now started for a raid westward along the Thames valley : the camps at Sinodun and Pusey, both large and formidable structures, possibly represent their halting-places on the first and second nights of their advance. The third day took them to Ashdown, in the "Vale of the White Horse." But they found there was still heavy fighting in prospect : the untiring Ethelred and Alfred had rallied their beaten host, and were now hanging on the invaders' heels and making it impossible for them to scatter after plunder. The heathen kings Halfdan and Bagsceg thereupon determined to take the offensive, and to attack and scatter the men of Wessex before proceeding farther with their raid. They were encamped high on the ridge of the Berkshire Downs, while Ethelred and Alfred lay at some distance below them.

Two such warriors as the sons of Ethelwulf were not likely to decline a fair battle in the open. When the Danes drew up in front of their camp

in two heavy bodies, the English arrayed themselves in two corresponding masses. It is now
that we get our first concrete and personal notice
of Alfred as warrior. His brother the king, pious
even to superstition as his father had been, lingered
behind in his camp hearing the mass. News was
brought him that the Danes were on the move,
but he swore that he would not leave his tent till
the priest had finished the last word of the service.
Alfred meanwhile, not less pious but more practical
than his brother, was in his proper place at the
head of his division. He waited long for Ethelred, but the king came not, and meanwhile the
Danes were drawing near, moving downward in
good order along the hillside. If they struck the
English host while it stood idly halted on the
lower slope, it was certain that they would bear it
down by their mere impetus. Then Alfred, taking
all the responsibility upon himself, ordered the
men of Wessex to advance up the ridge. The
four hostile divisions met with a great crash on the
down-side, where a single stunted thorn was long
pointed out as the actual spot of collision. The
struggle was long and fierce ; but Alfred, " pushing
uphill like a fierce wild boar," broke the Danish
line, and finally the invaders gave way and fled.
King Bagsceg and five earls, two Sihtrics, Osbiorn,
Fraena, and Harald were slain, with many thousands
of their men. Ethelred only arrived in time to

urge the pursuit, which was continued for two days, till King Halfdan and the wrecks of his host succeeded in sheltering themselves behind the palisades of their camp at Reading.

Western Christendom had won few such victories over its invaders ; yet all the fruits of the success vanished unaccountably in a few weeks. How it came to pass we cannot say, but only fourteen days after Ashdown another fight took place at Basing, a dozen miles south of Reading, and this time Ethelred was defeated. Two months later the war was still lingering on the borders of Berks and Wilts, and a battle was fought at Marton, near Bedwyn, in which Ethelred and Alfred were thoroughly beaten, and the king mortally wounded. He died at Eastertide, and his decease was at once followed by his brother's election to the throne (871).

Hitherto, save at Ashdown, it has been impossible to separate Alfred's doings from those of Ethelred. We may guess that much of the untiring energy shown by the men of Wessex was due to the activity of the Etheling rather than to that of his pious elder brother ; but we can prove nothing. When, however, Alfred begins to reign in his own right, we can at last make him personally responsible for the conduct of the war.

At first, it must be confessed, we can detect little more than mere courage and perseverance in the young king's conduct. Of generalship we find no evidence. His first battle was a disaster. The victors of Marton, strengthened by a large new "summer-army" from over-seas, pressed deeper into Wiltshire. Ere Alfred had been a month on the throne, he met them near Wilton, but his army was small. The spirit of Wessex had begun to fail after a year in which eight engagements with the invaders had already been fought, four of which had been bloody defeats. The thegnhood was terribly worn down in numbers, the shire-levies so discouraged that they came to the muster in number far smaller than usual. But Alfred nevertheless offered battle. Taking up a strong position on a hill, he repulsed the Danes with great slaughter when they attacked him. But his army, carried away by their ardour, charged down from its favourable post to cut up the defeated enemy. The Vikings rallied, and turned on their scattered pursuers, whom they finally drove from the field. Thus inauspiciously began Alfred's independent military career. But in spite of their victory the Danes, who had suffered almost as much as the English in this year of battles, consented to retire from Wessex on receiving a moderate sum of money. Alfred paid them, though he must have been aware that he was only buying a short respite. Time, however, was all-valuable to a king who wished to reorganise his exhausted realm.

For the next four years (872-875) there was comparative peace in Wessex : the enemy was employed partly on the Continent, partly in the conquest of Mercia, whose eastern half they annexed in 874, handing over the western part as a vassal kingdom to "an unwise thegn named Ceolwulf," who fondly thought that it was possible to settle down as a vassal of the greedy Northmen. Alfred's main endeavour in these years was to develop a navy ; he "built galleys and long-ships," and exerted himself to find trained crews for them, hiring "pirates"—converted Danes, we may suppose —to teach his own men seamanship. The beginnings of this national fleet must have been modest, for the chronicler thinks it a fact of note that the king's galleys were able in 875 to attack seven Viking ships, take one, and chase the rest out to sea. Two years later, however, the squadron, as we shall see from its doings, must have developed to a more formidable strength.

It was not till 876 that Alfred's reorganisation of his realm was put to the test. In that year a great Viking host under the kings Guthrum, Oskytel, and Amund made a sudden dash into Wessex, appeared in Dorsetshire, and seized Wareham, where they stockaded themselves between the Frome and the Trent in one of their usual water-girt camps. Alfred was soon upon them with the whole levy of Wessex, and held them so tightly blockaded—he made no attempt to storm their works after the experience of Reading—that they asked for terms, gave hostages, swore their greatest oath, and promised to depart. But when the king was off his guard all that part of the host that was provided with horses made a sudden sally, slipped through the English lines, and rode day and night till they reached Exeter, which they took by surprise. There they again stockaded themselves, and lay entrenched for the winter of 876-877. The indefatigable king followed them, again drew lines round their camp, and beleaguered them till they were oppressed with famine. They were depending for their relief on a squadron which was to run down the Channel and join them at the mouth of the Exe ; but Alfred sent his fleet, such as it was, to intercept the incoming pirates. There was an engagement somewhere off the south coast, from which the Danes retired without winning a victory, and immediately after a great storm cast their vessels on the cliffs of the Isle of Purbeck. A hundred and twenty galleys, with all their crews, are said to have perished near Swanage. Reduced to despair by this news, the Danes at Exeter asked for terms, and departed for Mercia before the summer was out.

This campaign had been such a complete success for Alfred that the events of the next year are a perfect surprise to us—as indeed they were to the contemporary observer ; "slay thirty thousand of these heathen in one day," says Asser, "and on the next sixty thousand will appear." In the first days of January 878 the main army of the Vikings, starting from Mercia, made a sudden and unexpected descent on Wiltshire, cutting the West-Saxon realm in twain. From a central camp at Chippenham they raided east and west into Hampshire on the one side and Somersetshire on the other. At the same time a separate pirate fleet which had spent its Yule in South Wales crossed the Bristol Channel and threw itself upon North Devon. It must have been the sudden and unexpected character of such an attack at mid-winter which for a moment seemed to have crushed Wessex. The king, who appears to have been in the west at the time, threw himself into the Isle of Athelney with a small band of his thegns and personal retainers, and there built his famous stockade in the marshes of the Parret. Elsewhere there was panic : many men of note fled over-seas to the Franks : large districts offered tribute and submission to the Danish king Guthrum.

But the worst of the panic only lasted a few weeks : before Easter the men of Devonshire rallied and cut to pieces at Kenwith the army from South Wales, slaying its leaders, Ingwar and Hubba, and 1200 of their followers, and capturing their famous Raven standard. Somewhat later the

levies of Somerset, Wilts, and Hampshire assembled
in the forest of Selwood under the king in person
and marched against the Danish camp at Chippenham.   The invaders, thinking they were strong
enough to fight in the open, moved out to Eddington to meet the advancing English.   There they
were routed in a battle of which we know no
details, save that the king's men fought in one
dense mass—not in two, as at Ashdown—and that
the fight was long and desperate.   The defeated
host fled to its stronghold at Chippenham, on the
east bank of the Avon.   Alfred followed hard
upon them, and, pushing up to the very gates of the
stockade, built a camp almost in actual touch with
it, so as to make any sortie well-nigh impossible.
The Danes were quite unprepared for a siege ;
they had fondly imagined that Wessex was their
own, and had accumulated no stores.   In fourteen
days they were starved out, and concluded with
the king the famous pact which is often, but inac-
curately, called the Peace of Wedmore.   King
Guthrum and thirty of his chiefs consented to
receive baptism, did homage to Alfred, and undertook to withdraw from his realm and to trouble
him no more.   These conditions, it is surprising to
find, were punctually fulfilled ; the Viking became
a Christian, and withdrew his host first to Ciren-
cester in Mercia and then to East Anglia, where
they all settled down and gave no trouble for some

years.   A great fleet which had come up the Thames as far as Fulham, and had been harassing Kent and Western Wessex, lingered some months after Guthrum's defeat, but gave up its enterprise in the spring of 879, sailed off eastwards, and set itself to ravage Flanders.

The peace of 878 is rightly taken as the turning-point of Alfred's reign.   He had so thoroughly impressed upon the Vikings the notion that in Wessex they would meet hard blows and small plunder that for some years they gave his realm a wide berth, and devoted their main attention to the Frankish kingdoms, where the imbecile Charles the Fat was just about to start upon his disgraceful career.   It was more profitable to blackmail realms whose kings shirked battles and proffered rich tribute than pay a visit to the indefatigable ruler of Wessex.   The events of 872-878 had made Alfred thoroughly well acquainted with every wile of Danish warfare ; he was not likely again to be taken by surprise, or caught unawares by an attack in time of truce or negotiation.   In the numerous wars of his later years he shows a mastery over his opponents which he was far from possessing in the days of Reading or Wilton.   In especial the great struggle of 893-896, when he had to face dangers quite as complicated and pressing as those of 872 or 878, found him so well prepared that its issue was never seriously in doubt, though the seat of war was perpetually shifting over every region between Kent and Chester, Essex and Exeter.

The first occupation to which Alfred seems to have devoted himself after the peace of 878 was the further development of his fleet. In 882 he actually went out with it in person and destroyed a small Viking squadron. In 885 he took the more daring step of sending it northward into hostile water. The East Anglian Danes having, after seven years of peace, broken their pact with him, he sent a squadron from Kent all up the Essex coast, and destroyed sixteen long-ships at the mouth of the Stour. Unfortunately his victorious vessels were intercepted by the whole force of the Danelagh ere they could return, and suffered a disastrous defeat. It was not till some years later, and when his last great war on land was over, that Alfred tried his final naval experiment, building " long-ships that were nigh twice as large as those of the Danes, some with sixty oars, some with more. They were both steadier and swifter, and also higher than others, and were shaped neither as the Frisian nor the Danish ships, but as it seemed to himself that they would be most handy." The natural result was the destruction of more than twenty Viking ships along the south coast in the sole summer of 897.

The second expedient which Alfred took in

hand was the systematic construction of fortifications. Not only were the towns encouraged to
surround themselves with strong ditches and palisades, but "burhs"—moated mounds girt with
concentric rings of ditch and stockade—were
erected at strategical points. London, recovered
from the East Anglian Danes in 886, was made
far stronger than it had ever been before by the
patching up of its ancient Roman walls. It was
filled with a new colony of warlike settlers, and
became an outpost of Wessex to the north of the
Thames. The consequences of the fact that the
larger English towns were no longer open but well
fortified are clearly seen in Alfred's later wars.
The Danes cannot capture important places at
the first rush, as they had done with York, Winchester, and London thirty years before. They
have to lay siege to them in full form, and always
before the siege is many days old the indefatigable
king appears with an army of relief. The invaders
had then either to fight, to take to their ships, or
to stockade themselves in their entrenchments and
suffer a leaguer themselves. Generally they chose
the second alternative, as at Rochester in 886,
when they abandoned their horses, their stores, and
all their heavy plunder, and sailed off the moment
that the army of succour came in sight. The
same scene occurred at Exeter in 894. The importance of fortified places in keeping the Danes

employed till the fyrd could assemble can hardly be exaggerated. The only stronghold which did not serve its purpose was a certain " work only half constructed in which there were some few country-folk " near Appledore in Kent. This fell before an attack of the " Great Army " in 893.

It would seem that the system by which Alfred's " burhs " were maintained was not unlike that which Henry the Fowler employed in Germany a generation later. To each stronghold there was allotted, as it would appear, a certain number of " hides " of land in the surrounding region. All the thegns dwelling on these hides were responsible for the defence of the burh. Probably they were bound to build a house within it, and either to dwell there in person, or to place therein a substitute equally competent with themselves for military purposes. It would seem that the " cnihten-guilds " of London and several other places were the original associations of these military settlers whom Alfred and his immediate successors placed in their burhs. Of the local distribution of the fortresses we have a precious relic in the " Burgal Hidage," a document belonging to the very early years of the tenth century, which gives a complete list of all the land dependent on the burhs of Wessex, and certain materials for the regions north of Thames also, where Edward the Elder was begin-ning to encroach on the Danelagh by means of his new foundations. That the system started with Alfred rather than his son seems to follow from two passages in the Anglo-Saxon Chronicle, where, under the year 894, we hear of " the king's thegns who were at home in the fortresses," and again of the fyrd being " half in the field and half at home, beside those men that held the burhs."

One of Alfred's devices of fortification deserves a special mention, as being new on this side of the Channel, though some partial precedents for it can be found in the wars of the Franks. In 896 the main body of the Viking invaders had concentrated at the Thames mouth, and then pushed up the river Lea to a spot fifteen miles from London, dragging their fleet with them. Noting the narrowness of the river, Alfred built two formidable burhs, one on each side of the Lea, just below the Danish camp, and then obstructed the stream —probably by palisades and floating booms— between the two forts. The hostile fleet was so securely " bottled up " that the Vikings had to abandon it when they moved off on land, and the Londoners were able to bring back the whole of the galleys to their city when the enemy was gone.

Beside the building of a fleet, and the systematic use of fortification, we have strong evidence that Alfred employed the third means of strengthening his realm that we indicated in the beginning of this chapter—that of increasing the numbers of the thegnhood, the professional military class. We are unfortunately not able to separate his work from that of his successor, Edward the Elder ; but as Alfred was a man of far more original genius than his son, we may fairly suspect him of being the originator of the scheme. It took the shape of enlisting in the ranks of the thegnhood all the more wealthy and energetic of the middle-classes both in the country-side and in the towns. Every ceorl who " throve so that he had fully five hides of land, and a helm and a mail-shirt, and a sword ornamented with gold," was to be for the future reckoned " gesithcund," or as another law phrased it, " of thegn-right worthy." A second draft of the first-quoted document even allows a ceorl who has the military equipment complete, but not fully the five hides of land, to slip into the privileged class. The same privilege was given—as a premium for energy among town-dwellers—to " the merchant who had fared thrice over the high seas at his own expense."

In return for their promotion in the social scale, ceorl and merchant alike were of course bound to follow the king to the field in full mail when he raised his banner, and no longer got off with the less arduous service expected from mere members of the shire-levy. We cannot doubt that such measures caused a large increase in the numbers of the thegnhood, and thereby provided the king with a more efficient and better armed core for the national host than his predecessors had ever possessed.

The campaigns against Hasting and the " Great Army " in 893-896 give, as we have already said, the best test of the efficiency of Alfred's reorganisation of his realm. The invaders came ashore in two places, Appledore in Kent and Milton by the Thames mouth. Each host found itself at once observed by a strong force, and unable to disperse for plunder. The king " encamped as near to them as he had room for the wood-fastnesses and the water-fastnesses, so that he might reach either if they might seek a field. Then they tried to go through the weald in troops, on whichever side there might not be a force. But each troop was sought out by a band from the king's host, and also from the burhs." At last the whole host at Appledore broke up and tried to march northward. Alfred stopped them at Farnham, took all their baggage, and drove them in disorder over the Thames. The survivors joined part of Hasting's army at Benfleet in Essex : the pirate king himself was absent with the rest. Following hard on their heels, the English stormed the camp, captured Hasting's wife and sons, and took a vast booty. But Alfred was not in person with this army : a third Viking host of a hundred ships had laid siege to Exeter, and he had flown westward to deal with it. On his approach the Vikings took to their ships and sailed up to the Channel and round the North Foreland to Shoeburyness in Essex, where they picked up the remnants of the force that had been routed at Benfleet, and some other reinforcements from the East Anglian Danes. Swelled to a large host by these accretions, the army that had failed at Exeter marched across Southern Mercia to the Severn, and " wrought a work " at Buttington.[1] Here they were at once beset by Alfred's son-in-law and most faithful servant, Ethelred Alderman of the Hwiccas, who had with him the levies of Somerset, Wilts, Gloucester, and Worcester. Expelled by him from the Severn valley, the Vikings retired to their kinsmen in Eastern England. There they again gathered reinforcements, and returning to the west, seized the empty walls of Chester—desolate since Ethelfrith had sacked the old Roman town in 606—and tried to establish themselves there. But again they had no rest : the forces of English Mercia, aided by the kings of North Wales, laid siege to the place. Starvation finally compelled the Vikings to abandon it. They went back through the friendly territory of their Northumbrian kinsmen, and returned to East Anglia (895). Their last effort was made in the following year, and consisted in the advance up the Thames and Lea which we have already had

---

[1] In Shropshire, and not to be identified with Boddington in Gloucestershire.

occasion to describe. There King Alfred assailed them in person, and captured their fleet by the device of blocking the river by his two burhs. Deprived of their vessels the Danes made their last march : pressing overland, they for the second time entered the Severn valley and "wrought a work" at Quatbridge.[1] Alfred followed them with the bulk of his host, and lay opposite them as the winter set in. It was impossible to get away from this untiring pursuer, and in the next spring the "Great Army" broke up in despair : "some returned to East Anglia and some to Northumbria, and those that were moneyless got themselves ships and went south over sea to the Seine. Thanks be to God, the army had not broken up the English race" (896).

These splendid campaigns, known to us, alas ! only in outline, are the finest testimony to Alfred's powers of organisation that could be given. Wherever the Vikings appeared they were at once met by a sufficient force and held in check. Their strong camps could not defend them as of old : sometimes the palisades were stormed, sometimes blockade did the work, and the host had to depart in order to save itself from starvation. Three years of perpetual disaster tired out at last even the obstinacy of the battle-loving Northmen. They dispersed and sought other scenes of activity and

[1] Now Quatford, in Shropshire, like their former stronghold at Buttington.

enemies less formidable than the great king of Wessex.

For the last four years of his life Alfred was undisturbed save by trifling raids of small squadrons, which he brushed off with ease by means of the new fleet of " great ships " which he had built. The work of defence was done : Wessex was saved, and with Wessex the English nationality. In a few years the king's gallant son, Edward the Elder, was to take the offensive against the old enemy, and to repay on the Danelagh all the evils that England had suffered during the miserable years of the ninth century. That such triumphs lay within his power was absolutely and entirely the work of his great father, who had turned defeat into victory, brought order out of chaos, and left the torn and riven kingdom that he had inherited transformed into the best organised and most powerful state in Western Europe.

ALFRED AS A GEOGRAPHER

By Sir Clements Markham

ALFRED AS A GEOGRAPHER

THE single-minded devotion of King Alfred to the service of his people is shown in every action of his life ; and one of the greatest, certainly the most remarkable undertaking for that end, was the conveyance of knowledge to them in their own language, through paraphrased translations. It was thus that he strove to disseminate some acquaintance with theology, moral philosophy, history, and geography. It is a very striking and suggestive fact that a ruler who surpassed all others that the world has ever seen in wisdom and insight, as well as in complete abnegation of every selfish thought in his dealings with his people, should have given so high a place to geography. Alfred knew by experience that an acquaintance with the relative positions of places on the earth's surface was the necessary foundation of the kind of knowledge required equally by the statesman,

the soldier, and the merchant ; and he therefore gave its due place to geography in his grand scheme for the enlightenment of Englishmen.   In this he was centuries in advance of his age, and even now the standard in this, as in other respects, is below that of the wisest of our kings.

Alfred, as was his wont, when he had resolved to bring knowledge on any particular subject within the reach of his people, diligently sought out the best authority on geography.   Ptolemy, Strabo, and Pliny were unknown to his generation, still hidden away in dark repositories and not to be unearthed until the dawn of the Renaissance.   In the ninth century the best geographical work was that of Paulus Orosius, who had lived in the days of the Emperor Honorius.   He was a native of Tarragona in Spain, and took orders in the Christian church.   Perplexed by the controversies in his own country, the young Spanish deacon undertook a voyage to Africa, to receive the solution of his doubts from the famous Bishop of Hippo.   Orosius secured the friendship of St. Augustine, who sent him to Palestine on two occasions before A.D. 416, and gave him opportunities for study.   The result was a work intended to refute the pagan opinion that the sack of Rome by Alaric was due to the anger of the ancient gods.   It, however, contained much more than mere polemics, and was in fact a summary of the world's history from the creation to the days of Honorius, with a sketch of all that was then known of geography.

Alfred brought high qualifications to the task of translating and editing Orosius.[1] In his boyhood he had twice made journeys to Rome, which, as regards danger and hardships, may be compared to an expedition to Lhasa at the present day. In after life he had become very intimately acquainted with the topography of his native island, from the Humber to the shores of the Channel, and from the Severn to the East Anglian coast. As a military tactician he knew each river, valley, hill range, and plain ; as an administrator he had examined the capabilities of every district ; and as a naval commander, the harbours and estuaries, the tides and currents were familiar to him. So far as his personal knowledge extended, Alfred was a trained geographer. He was also in a position to increase the information derived from his own personal experiences by diligently collecting materials from those foreigners who frequented his court, and by reading. He had the gift of assimilating the knowledge thus acquired, and he studied most diligently. Above all, he was eager to in-

---

[1] The manuscripts of Alfred's *Orosius* are in the Cottonian collection and in the Lauderdale MS. They were used by Hakluyt. The work was first edited by Daines Barrington and Reinhold Foster in 1773 ; and in 1855 a literal English translation, with a facsimile, and the Anglo-Saxon text, were published by the Rev. Joseph Bosworth, D.D.

vestigate unknown things for the great end he always had in view—the good of his people.

Alfred's design was to collect the best and most extensive geographical information, without confining himself to the text of Orosius. Thus he commences his geographical work with a very lucid account of the peoples of central Europe and of their relative positions, which is not in the work of Orosius, but was composed by the king himself from his own sources of information. It is the only account from which such details in that age can be derived.

The East Franks, he tells us, were established east of the Rhine and north of the source of the Danube. The Swabians were to the south and beyond the Danube, while the Bavarians were farther east round the town of Ratisbon, both peoples occupying the country up to the foot of the Alps. East of the Bavarians was Bohemia, and to the north-east was Thuringia. Turning to the north of Germany the king places the old Saxons round the mouth of the Elbe, and the Frisians farther west. North of the Elbe were the Angles, who nearly all came to people England, and the Danes on the mainland and in the island of Zeeland. King Alfred then gives some details respecting the Slavonic tribes in the eastern part of Germany. The Afdrede were established in what is now Mecklenburg, and the Wylte in that part of the mark of Brandenburg then called Hæfeldan. The Sysyle were in a part of Eastern Prussia then known as Wineda-land. Eastward from the countries of the Bohemians and Bavarians were the Moravians; and to the south, beyond the Danube again, and extending to the Alps, was Carinthia. A desert, by which the Karst may be intended, extended between Carinthia and the land of the Bulgarians, beyond which was the Byzantine empire. To the east of Moravia was Wisl-land, the region watered by the Vistula, Dalamensan, Horithi, and Surpe. These Slavonic peoples occupied Poland, and to the north-east was Sermende, the modern Livonia.

Having given the relative positions of the peoples inhabiting central Europe, King Alfred turns to the north, and takes us to the countries bordering on the British sea and the Baltic, or Ost-sæ as he calls it. The north Danes were then in the provinces of Halland and Scania, now part of Sweden, as well as in the islands. To the eastward were the Afdrede already mentioned as occupying Mecklenburg, the Burgendas apparently on the island of Bornholm, and Osti or Easterlings, a Finnish race, inhabited Esthonia. On the Scandinavian peninsula were the Sweon or Swedes, the Northmen, and the Scride-Finnas or "striding Finns." Far to the north, between the Gulf of Bothnia and the Arctic Sea, including Finmarken, was the waste country called Cwenland.

Having given this most valuable summary of the inhabitants of Central and Northern Europe during the ninth century, King Alfred proceeds to relate the particulars of two important voyages made by distinguished seamen who had come to his court and recited their adventures to him. The first was an influential Northman or Norwegian named Oht-here, or in old Norwegian, Ottar. The name is derived from the two words *oht* (dread or fear) and *hær* or *here* (an army), *hærmand*, a warrior. The right meaning of Oht-here is, therefore, " terror-causing warrior." This able navigator "told his Lord King Alfred that he dwelt northmost of all Northmen, on the land by the west sea." The district in which he dwelt was called Halgoland, the land of fire, or more probably " the land of the northern lights." Oht-here's home has been placed on the shores of Lerivik Sound, between the Island of Senjen and the main-land. " He said no man abode north of him. He was a wealthy man in those possessions in which their wealth consists," possessing 600 tame reindeer of his own breeding, 20 horned cattle, as many sheep and swine, and horses with which he ploughed a small extent of tilled land. But his revenues were chiefly derived from tribute paid to him by the Laplanders, called Finns by the Norwegians, in furs and skins, birds' feathers, whalebone, and ropes made from walrus hide.   Oht-here called his country Northweg (Norway), and described it as being very long and narrow, with all the pasture and culturable land near the sea, which, however, is very rocky in some places.   Inland, he said that there were high mountains, and farther to the eastward were Sweden in the south and Cwenland in the north.   He added that to the north of Halgoland the country was waste and desert, except in a few places, where the Laplanders were encamped for hunting, or on the sea-coast for fishing in the summer.

Oht-here was evidently a man of high position and great influence, one who was worthy of the friendship and confidence of King Alfred.   He was inspired by the noble desire for Arctic exploration and discovery, or, as he expressed himself to the king, he desired to find out how the land lay far to the north.   So he undertook a most adventurous voyage to the northward, coasting along the land, keeping the wild, rocky coast on his starboard side and the wide Arctic Sea on what he called his *bæc-bord*.   Continuing this course for three days, he passed beyond the most northern point to which the whale-hunters ever went in those days.   Still pressing onwards, he attained the most northern point ever reached by man, in about 71° 15′ N The land then trended eastward, and, after waiting a short time for a westerly wind, he shaped a course along the coast to the eastward until he reached the entrance of the White Sea on the fourth day. Here he waited for a northerly breeze, which enabled him to coast round the Kola peninsula to the mouth of the Varzuga river, and thus to discover the White Sea. Here he stopped owing to fear of hostilities from the natives beyond. These were the North Carelians, on the western coast of the White Sea. Oht-here calls them Beormas, and says that they had a well-peopled land.

Oht-here's discoveries included the whole of the Arctic coast of Finmarken and the shores of the White Sea as far as the mouth of the Varzuga. He was the first to double the North Cape, and Oht-here's farthest north held its ground for nearly seven hundred years, until the voyage of Willoughby and Chancellor in 1553.

Oht-here calls the country between the Gulf of Bothnia and the Arctic Sea, Terfinna land, *Ter* being the ancient name of the Kola peninsula. Terfinna therefore means the Finns in Ter. He describes it as entirely waste and uninhabited, except where the Laplanders were encamped for hunting or fishing. He was told many tales respecting their country by the Beormas, but King Alfred did not record them, because they were only from hearsay, and not things the explorer could testify to from personal knowledge.

Besides discovery, another object of Oht-here's voyage was the capture of walrus, for the sake of their hides and tusks. He calls the walrus a horse whale, but says that it is much smaller than other whales ; thus correctly including whales, usually supposed to be fish in ancient times, under the head of mammalia, by classing them with the walrus. The length of a walrus is given, with approximate accuracy, at 14 feet. Oht-here told King Alfred that the great whales were from 96 to 100 feet long, and that the best whale-hunting was off his own country of Halgoland. The skill and energy of those old Norsemen must have been most remarkable, for Oht-here says that his was one of six vessels which killed sixty whales in two days. The ships must have had very large crews, and a considerable number of boats for each ship, to have achieved such an unequalled feat, probably without a rival in the whole history of whaling. But it is more likely that Oht-here alluded to walrus or " horse whales."

Oht-here also described to the king a voyage to the south from Halgoland, along the coast of Norway, to Denmark and Slesvig. He said that with a fair wind, and anchoring each night, the voyage from Halgoland to a port he calls Sciringe-sheal, might be made in a month. Sciringesheal is in old Norwegian *Scirings-salr*, which, in the ninth century, was a town on the shores of a small bay in Larviks-fjord, called Viks-fjord. In the English of Alfred the termination *salr* (a large room) is changed into *heal* (a hall). On the *bæc-bord* is Norway, and on the starboard side is Iraland and other islands. He then describes a great sea running inland, the Kattegat and the Baltic, with Jutland and Zeeland on the other side. The Baltic, he adds, runs several hundred miles up into the land. Oht-here sailed from Sciringesheal southwards, through the Danish islands to the coast of Slesvig, and reached the port of Haddeby. Alfred adds the interesting fact that the Angles dwelt in these lands round Haddeby before they came into England.

Oht-here made a present of walrus ivory to King Alfred ; but he was not the only adventurous seaman who brought welcome information to the king. A Dane named Wulfstan gave him an account of a voyage in the Baltic from Haddeby to Truso, in what is now Eastern Prussia, and described to him the manners and customs of the people he visited.

Haddeby, mentioned both by Oht-here and Wulfstan, was no doubt an important trading port in the ninth century. The word, as given by Alfred, is *æt Hæthum*, meaning "at the Heaths." "The town at the heaths" is the same as Hedeby or Haddeby, the ancient name of Slesvig. It is now a pretty little village, with a very ancient granite church, on the banks of the river Schley, just opposite the more recent town of Slesvig. Wulfstan made the voyage from Haddeby to Truso in seven days. He had the Danish islands on the *bæc-bord*, and the land of the Wends, now Mecklenburg, and Pomerania on his starboard side ; then the Swedish provinces of Bleking and Smaland, and the isles of Bornholm, Öland, and Gothland, to the north ; and the mouth of the Vistula to the south. Wulfstan finished his voyage by entering the inland sea, called Frische Haff, by a narrow strait, and going up the Elbing river to the town of Truso on the Drausen lake in East Prussia.

Wulfstan gave a very full account of this country of Estum or Esthonia to King Alfred. There are kings in every town, he says, and the richer folk drink mare's milk (probably the fermented *kumiss* made from milk), while the poor people drink mead. The custom of treating their dead is to keep the bodies preserved in ice for a long time before they are burnt, during which there is drinking and festivities. The dead man's property is then divided into several lots, and placed along a course to be raced for, so that swift horses become uncommonly dear. King Alfred was also much struck by Wulfstan's account of the way in which the Esthonians could produce cold, both for preserving the dead during the period of festivities, and for icing their liquors.

In recording the information received from his two sailor visitors, Oht-here and Wulfstan, the clearness and perspicacity of the narrative, and the rejection of all hearsay evidence, show that King Alfred was most careful and conscientious, anxious to secure accuracy, and only to present to his people what was reliable.   The voyages themselves are interesting, because they prove that, although the seas were alive with the piratical fleets of Rolf the Ganger, Hasting, and many other warriors bent only on pillage and rapine, there were at the same time peaceful ventures and even expeditions of discovery.

The first voyage of Oht-here is memorable as the first Arctic expedition undertaken for the sake of discovery and exploration.   There is nothing to show that it was undertaken under the auspices, or even with the knowledge, of Alfred.   But it is certain that it received the cordial approval of our great king, and that its motives had the sympathy and appreciation of one who, in regenerating the navy of England, knew well that such training was of vital importance to a naval power.   The welcome he extended to his Arctic visitor, and the care with which he elicited his information and recorded it, leave no doubt of what Alfred's feelings were upon this subject.   When it is remembered that Alfred the Great rebuilt the English navy from his own designs, improving upon the lines of

Danish and Norse ships, it ought not to be for-gotten, in the same connection, how highly he valued the work of Arctic exploration. He at least knew that a training in deeds of seaman-like daring and adventure is as important as the building of ships for securing and maintaining power on the sea. We have no further knowledge of the personal intercourse between the first Arctic ex-plorer and " his Lord King Alfred." He was cordially received at the English court, he pre-sented the king with an offering of walrus ivory, and there must have been conversations in the course of which the king received and sifted the evidence of his guest, until he was able to record the lucid and accurate narrative which has been preserved and handed down to us.

After recording the events of the voyages of Oht-here and Wulfstan, King Alfred returns to the text of Orosius, where the geography of Greece and the islands is discussed, as well as that of the countries on the shores of the Adriatic. Thence Orosius passes to Italy, France, and Spain ; and in the latter country Cadiz and Betanzos in Galicia are mentioned. France was personally known to Alfred, who had visited the court of Charles the Bald, but he gives no reminiscence of his journeys. Nearly all Spain was then under the enlightened rule of the powerful western Khalifas Almondhir and Abdallah, while the Christian kings of Oviedo fought to maintain a struggling existence in the mountains of Asturias. Even Leon was not occupied by them until after the death of Alfred. In his reference to Britain and the surrounding islands, including the Orkneys, there is an allusion to "the uttermost land that men call Thule," north-west of Ireland. Alfred held it to be Iceland, apparently.

Africa is then treated of, with rather more fulness. The positions of Egypt and Libya Cyrenaica, of the Nasamones, near the Syrtis Major, of Numidia, Mauritania, and the Atlas Mountains, are laid down; and after a passage where Orosius remarks on the ingratitude of the Egyptians to the memory of Joseph, King Alfred inserts an interesting reflection of his own: "So also it is still in all the world. If God for a very long time grants any one his will, and he then takes it away for a less time, he soon forgets the good which he had before, and thinks only upon the evil which he then hath."

The concluding part of the work refers to the Mediterranean islands. Sicily is described with its three points, Pelorus, Pachynum, and Lilybæum; but there is a serious mistake as regards its size, perhaps due to an error in transcription. Finally, there are notices of Scythia and Bactria, of Arabia and India, of Palestine and the Jordan, and of Cilicia, Isauria, and other places in Asia Minor, this part being from the text of Orosius.   Africa seems to have been conceived to be a long, narrow continent, smaller than Europe, with no very great extension towards the south.

When we consider the ignorance which prevailed in England before Alfred's time, we can form an idea of the immense importance of his geographical labours and of the brightness of the light with which he dispelled outer darkness in the minds of his countrymen.   His work was more especially useful in his own time, owing to the intercourse he encouraged with foreign lands, and to the frequent missions he despatched and received.   Every year there was intercourse with Rome, when the alms for St. Peter were despatched, generally in charge of an alderman or a dignitary of the Church. Embassies were received from Germany and the northern countries, from France, and probably from the Emperor Leo the Philosopher at Constantinople, and from the great western Khalifa at Cordova.   King Alfred even despatched a mission to India, at the head of which was Sighelm or Suithelm, the Bishop of Sherburn.   In those days there were native dynasties at the principal seats of Hindu civilisation.   The Chohan kings were reigning at Delhi and Ajmir.   At Ujjayana the Malwa Rajas held a brilliant court, where literature flourished, and where Kalidasa and his school reached the highest flights of poetic imagination.

At Madura, in Southern India, was the cultured Pandyon dynasty. It is probable that the visit of King Alfred's envoy was to the Pandyon King of Madura, for his instructions were to seek out the shrine of St. Thomas, which has traditionally been placed on the Coromandel coast. It is recorded that the Bishop of Sherburn returned safely to England, bringing back with him gems and other products of a country which was destined, in after ages, to become the brightest gem in the diadem of the descendants of Alfred the Great.

Both through his promotion of intercourse with distant lands and through his literary work, our great king enlightened his people by disseminating geographical knowledge. The first to encourage Arctic exploration, the first to point the way to eastern trade by the Baltic, the first to open communication with India, his literary labours in the cause of geography are even more astonishing. There have been literary sovereigns since the days of Timæus of Sicily, writing for their own glory or for their own edification or amusement. Alfred alone wrote with the sole object of his people's good ; while in his methods, in his scientific accuracy, and in his aims, he was several centuries in advance of his time. After his death there was a dreary waste of ignorance, with scarcely even a sign of dawn on the distant horizon. A few Englishmen of ability, such as Roger Bacon and

Sacrobosco, speculated and wrote on questions "*de sphærâ*," but there was no practical geography until Eden and Hakluyt rose up, nearly seven centuries after the death of our great king. Richard Hakluyt was indebted to Alfred for portions of his work, and he resembled his illustrious precursor somewhat in his zeal, his patriotism, and his diligence. Hakluyt was, however, far behind Alfred in scientific precision and insight, although he lived so long afterwards, with seven more centuries of experience to guide him. Even now men of learning and research have their admiration aroused at the accuracy of King Alfred's descriptions, and at the pains he must have taken to reject what was doubtful and to retain only what was true. This called for the exercise of ability of a high order, as well as patience.

Alfred the Great was, in the truest sense of the term, a man of science; and we hail him as one who stands alone and unrivalled—the founder of the science of geography in this country.

ALFRED AS A WRITER

By Rev. Professor Earle

ALFRED AS A WRITER

OUR estimate of the literary achievements of King Alfred will depend very much upon what we are in the habit of thinking about his early education. If we are content to accept the story in Asser, that he had reached his twelfth year before he had learned to read, then we must reckon his literary career as a prodigy, a phenomenon which defies explanation. Or, if that will not satisfy us, we may liken him to his grandfather's contemporary the great Charles, who, being illiterate, knew the value of learning, and surrounded himself with learned men. On this theory it would follow that the writings of King Alfred are his only in that sense in which all works and monuments are said to belong to the king who has ordered them and paid for them. He who refuses to be satisfied with either of these alternatives can hardly fail to question the story about Alfred and the picture-book.

The Saxon Chronicle says that Alfred was sent

to Rome in the year 853, at which time he was a little boy. This statement naturally suggests that he was sent to reside at the English College in Rome for the benefit of his education. But this is blurred in Asser by the further statement that he went to Rome a second time in the very next year ; which has the effect of reducing his travels to mere excursions. The second journey to Rome is not in the Chronicle, and it looks rather like an artifice, designed to parry the natural inference that the journey to Rome was for a prolonged and educational residence. Perhaps the author of " Asser's Life " was minded to make his hero a prodigy, and to this end the picture-book story must by all means be protected and maintained. These variations had the effect of shaking the credibility of the narrative, and raising doubts as to whether Alfred ever went to Rome at all. The statement in the Chronicle got involved in that cloud of unreality which overshadows so much of Alfred's history.

Happily this particular point is now quite cleared up. A letter has been discovered, written by Leo IV., the reigning Pope in the year 853, and addressed to King Æthelwulf, the father of Alfred, announcing the safe arrival of the boy. This discovery has added a new confirmation to the Chronicle, and has established it once for all as a firm historical fact, that Alfred was sent to Rome in the year 853.   If now we interpret this step in the most natural manner, as designed by his father to send the child out of the way in dangerous times, and to occupy his tender years with liberal studies, we find the course of Alfred's literary development well and reasonably accounted for.   Indeed, it seems in every way most probable that Alfred enjoyed the best opportunities for study that the times afforded, and that he used them so far as was compatible with the vocation of a warrior.   How many years he spent in Rome is not known ; in the reign of Æthered he was at home and he made a conspicuous military figure while yet in his teens, and this seems to indicate that he had never in his book-learning forgotten that he would have to fight for his country against the northern invaders.

The first seven years of his own reign (871-878) were years of deadly struggle.   In 877 his cause seemed to be lost, but in 878 the King of Wessex was victorious.   He made peace with the conquered Danes, and their king, Guthrum, was baptized.   And now he had to guide in peace the nation which he had guided in war.   He had to reconstruct the social and political fabric which had been shattered by the devastations and panics of three generations.   In all his reconstruction there is manifested a purpose not only of restoration, but also of improvement and reform.   This is conspicuous in his revision of the West Saxon

Laws.   The Law-book then in use was that of King
Ina (688-726). When Alfred's code was published,
that of Ina was not abolished, but it was re-edited
in the same volume, after the manner of an appendix
to Alfred's Laws.   That a new departure was
purposed is indicated by the new feature of a
Prologue composed of the Decalogue and kindred
selections from Scripture.   This is to be understood partly as a consecration of the new Law-
book ; but further, as the inauguration of a new
principle, namely, that laws are founded in right
reason and have their highest sanction in religion.
Before Alfred's time laws had rested upon tradition, deriving their force from the fact that they
were ancestral, or if reasoned at all were based upon
a stunted and barbaric type of reasoning.   We
happen to have an extant example in which we can
compare a law of Ina's with Alfred's reform of it.
In the case of damage to a wood, the old law drew
a distinction between injury by fire and injury by
the axe, and that by fire was punished far more
heavily than the other, for this assigned reason—that
fire is a thief and works silently, whereas the axe
announces itself.

" In case any one burn a tree in a wood, and it
come to light who did it, let him pay the full
penalty, let him give sixty shillings, because fire is
a thief. If one fell in a wood ever so many trees,
and it be found out afterwards, let him pay for

three trees, each with thirty shillings.   He is not required to pay for more of them, however many they might be, because the axe is a reporter and not a thief (forðon seo æsc biþ melda, nalles ðeof)."

This contrast could be retorted : for it might be urged that if fire is a thief relatively to the owner of the wood, so is it also relatively to the defendant, for it had started up afresh when he had left the place thinking that all was safe.   The worst that could be proved upon him was the want of *sufficient* caution.   In fact, the law is only good as against arson, wanton or malicious ; and for that case it is not severe enough.   It may be assumed that in the bulk of cases damage by fire would be undesigned and accidental.

But where the axe is used there can be no doubt about the motive.   The man who fells another man's timber does so plainly with intent to steal, and the noise of the axe is not extenuating but rather aggravating by reason of its audacity.

In Ina's law all such considerations were prevented by two venerable maxims which said, "Fire is a thief, but the axe is outspoken."   Jacob Grimm, in his *Antiquities of Law*, produced some parallels from old German codes, but he gave the palm to this of ours for its poetic tinge.   Moreover, as an indication of the national instinct which is favourable to whatever is open and straightfor-

ward, it may be interesting ; but the distinction
was bad as law, and it was abolished by King
Alfred.   His new law equalised the penalty thus :
" If a man burn or hew another man's wood without leave, let him pay for every great tree with
five shillings, and afterwards for each, let there be
ever so many, with five pence ;—and a fine of thirty
shillings."

The closing words of the king's Prologue are
as follows :—

" I, Alfred the King, gathered these (laws) together and ordered many to be written which our
forefathers held, such as I approved, and many
which I approved not I rejected, and had other
ordinances enacted with the counsel of my Witan ;
for I dared not venture to set much of my own
upon the statute-book, for I knew not what might
be approved by those who should come after us.
But such ordinances as I found, either in the time
of my kinsman Ina, or of Offa, King of the Mercians, or of Ethelberht, who first received baptism
in England—such as seemed to me rightest I have
collected here, and the rest I have let drop.

" I, then, Alfred, King of the West Saxons,
showed these laws to all my Witan, and they then
said that they all approved of them as proper to
be holden."

The same spirit of improvement and vigorous
initiative is manifested in his famous translations.

THE SEASONS—JULY TO SEPTEMBER

Either by his own knowledge or by the good advice which he knew how to obtain and appreciate, he selected from the books then accessible those which were calculated to be most generally useful to his people. The chief books were five, the productions of four authors : one by Orosius, written about A.D. 412 ; one by Boethius, of about A.D. 522 ; two by Gregory the Great, written towards A.D. 600 ; and one by the Venerable Bede, which was brought to a close in the year 731. It may be useful to add a few particulars about each of the works which appear to have constituted the select library of King Alfred.

Orosius was a young priest who came out of Spain into Africa to visit Augustine, Bishop of Hippo, at the time when that Father of the Latin Church was writing his greatest work, which he entitled the *City of God*. The occasion for this work arose out of the sack of Rome by Alaric the Goth in the year 410. A great outcry was made by the pagans against Christianity, as if it had been the cause of calamities which they attributed to the displeasure of the ancient gods for their neglected altars. In his *City of God*, which was conceived as an answer to this charge, Augustine constructed his argument upon a broad view of human history, urging that events must not be interpreted in an isolated manner, but must be taken with their connection and sequence ; and then we shall discern signs of a great providential purpose guiding mankind in a progressive course of amelioration. The old dispensation prepared men for a fuller revelation, and the spread of Christianity has brought manifest improvement in the condition of human life. The heathen empires of the world, as Babylon in the East and Rome in the West, have been active though unconscious factors in this vast and beneficent process. The book is in fact a philosophy of history, with the Gospel for its pivot, and all events subordinated to this master principle. The thesis is developed with an extraordinary wealth of reasoning and illustration. To make this great argument the more complete, Orosius undertook, at Augustine's request, to write a compendium of general history in the same spirit, and accordingly he loses no opportunity of showing up the calamities of the old heathen times, and indicating the tendency of Christianity to mitigate the horrors of war. This book of Orosius became the recognised manual of general history down to the sixteenth century.

The *Consolation of Philosophy* by Boethius was the chief if not the sole representative of the philosophy, the ethics, and the religious aspirations of the ancients during the Dark and early Middle Ages. The author is thus introduced by Gibbon : " The senator Boethius is the last of the Romans whom Cato or Tully could have acknowledged for their countryman." Suspected by Theodoric, the Gothic King of Italy, of the crime of Roman patriotism, he was cast into prison, and a sentence of confiscation and death was pronounced against him, while he was denied the means of making his defence. Chained and in view of death he composed the *Consolation of Philosophy*, of which Gibbon says : " A golden volume, not unworthy of the leisure of Plato or Tully, but which claims incomparable merit from the barbarism of the times and the situation of the author." [1]

Gregory the Great, who in A.D. 597 sent Augustine with his missionary band to the King of Kent, is a name which through the whole extent of Anglo-Saxon literature is mentioned with a peculiar veneration. From his writings the king took two books to be included in his library of English translations. The first was his *Pastoral Care (Cura Pastoralis)*, a guide-book for the use of the priest, to instruct the consciences of those who come to him for spiritual counsel ; and as it is the first, so it may safely be pronounced the best of all manuals of the kind. Gregory's ideal is

---

[1] It is a noted character of this book that while it contains much that is acceptable to the Christian spirit and nothing that is repugnant to it, there is not a word in it which might not have been written by a pagan of the sixth century who had inherited the influences of centuries of Christianity. Those who desire to know more about Boethius, and the various ancient translations of his last work, and his influence upon mediæval thought, and the controversies of which he has been the occasion, should consult *Boethius, An Essay*, by Hugh Fraser Stewart, M.A. ; Blackwood and Son, 1891.

a world governed by conscience, and the spirit of the *Cura Pastoralis* would transform all men into worthy citizens of such a polity.

The other book of Gregory's which Alfred took was of a different kind. The *Dialogues* are stories of a sensational or even grotesque character, with a religious moral. They are calculated for a childish level of intelligence, and were designed to compete with the degrading tales which were the entertainment of barbarian circles. This book, which enjoyed the highest popularity for centuries, and was among the earliest books to be printed, is now entirely neglected, and Alfred's translation has not yet been edited.

Bede was born in the neighbourhood of Wearmouth in 672. In his seventh year he entered the abbey recently founded there by Benedict Biscop, who was the first abbot. In that and the sister house of Jarrow he continued to his death in 735. He wrote *Historia Ecclesiastica Gentis Anglorum*, the History of the Conversion of the Angles and Saxons and of their Earliest Ecclesiastical Institutions. No other national church possesses a history of equal merit.[1] This was the youngest book on Alfred's list, and as Orosius

---

[1] The only one to be compared with it is the *History of Early Frankish Christianity*, by Gregory, the Bishop of Tours, with which, indeed, it has been compared by Canon Bright, and the comparison is made in a generous spirit.

was, what Pauli calls it,[1] a Chronicle of the World, so this was a History of England.

I have thus endeavoured to give some idea of the books chosen by Alfred, as regards their rank and place in general literature. Our next step is to consider how Alfred dealt with these books and what he made of them. In his mind the translator's function was not to reproduce an ancient author, but to produce a useful work. How he treated Orosius may readily be seen by any one who will examine the latest edition of the translation, that by Dr. Sweet (Early English Text Society). He hit upon the admirable plan of printing opposite the translation the corresponding portions of the Latin text, using italics for such parts of the original as are not literally translated. How great was the freedom of adaptation is promptly seen by the swarms of italics with which the Latin pages are bespangled. Besides these adaptations there are substantial additions in the shape of original contributions by King Alfred to the knowledge of European geography. First there is a map-like description of the nations of Central and Northern Europe, which are comprised under the name of Germania. The author begins with

---

[1] *König Ælfred und seine Stelle in der Geschichte Englands,* von Dr. Reinhold Pauli, Berlin, 1851. *The Life of Alfred the Great.* Translated from the German of Dr. R. Pauli. To which is appended Alfred's Anglo-Saxon version of Orosius. With a literal English translation, etc. London, 1853. (Bohn's Antiquarian Library.)

a sketch of his area : by east and west, from the
Don to the sea about Britain ; by north and south,
from the Danube and Euxine to the White Sea.
Coming to details, he starts with the East Franks
(whose land-mark and memorial now lives in
Frankfort), and with these East Franks for a
centre he gives the relative positions of Swabians,
Bavarians, Bohemians, and Thuringians, to the
north of whom lie the Old Saxons, who are bounded
on the west by Elbe-mouth and Friesland.   From
this point the Old Saxons become the pivot of the
description.

This new piece of geographical literature is
followed by two narratives of northern voyagers :
Oht-here, who had explored the coast of Norway
from where is now Christiania to far round the
North Cape ; and Wulfstan, who explored the
southern coasts of the Baltic, and describes the
strange customs of the Esthonians.

These three pieces taken together constitute one
homologous group of ninth-century geography,
which fully justifies Reinhold Pauli's estimate, that
the " Germania " of Alfred is more extensive and
better defined than the "Germania" of Tacitus.

Besides this large insertion there are several
smaller ones in the course of the work, and these
may easily be found by observing where blanks
occur on the Latin page of Dr. Sweet's edition.
Where Orosius tells how M. Fabius refused a

Triumph when it was offered to him by the Senate, the translator inserts two paragraphs, one describing a Roman Triumph, and the other relating the origin and functions of the Roman Senate. In Cæsar's invasion of Britain, where Orosius tells how he reached the river Thames, which (says he) is fordable in one place only ; the translator adds that the ford is now called Wallingford. In such occasional insertions we see the beginnings of that vast apparatus of modern learning which is now relegated to footnotes or to separate books of reference.

The conditions under which Boethius produced that unique work *The Consolation of Philosophy* may have tended to give the book a special attraction for the mind of the trouble-tossed king. He certainly seems to have made great use of the book as a text for his own reflections and meditations. " For although King Alfred professed to translate the work of Boethius, yet he inserted in various parts many of his own thoughts and feelings," etc. These are the words of one who up to the moment of writing was the latest editor of Alfred's *Boethius* ;[1] but now he must share the ground with Mr. Sedgefield, whose new and greatly improved text has just issued from the Clarendon Press. On

---

[1] *King Alfred's Anglo-Saxon Version of Boethius,* etc. By the Rev. Samuel Fox, M.A., 1864. (Bohn's Antiquarian Library.) This book will continue to be in request, because of the translation which faces the Anglo-Saxon text.

Alfred's manner of dealing with his originals Mr. Sedgefield says : " Even in his most faithful translation, that of the *Cura Pastoralis*, King Alfred is by no means what in these days would be called literal ; while in his *Boethius* it is the exception to find a passage of even a few lines rendered word for word." And, we may add, it is precisely this free handling which gives to the king's translations their personal interest, and nowhere is this peculiar attraction so strongly felt as in his adaptation of Boethius.

German research has somewhat modified the inference which ascribed to Alfred everything in his version which is not found in the text. Old Latin commentaries and scholia upon the *De Consolatione* have been discovered in continental libraries, which contain similar expansions, especially those in the direction of Christian doctrine. This discovery enlarges the literary interest, with small detraction from the work of the king. His glory is not of a kind to rise and fall by little gradations of more or less. The suggestions supplied by these commentaries are in their nature very obvious. For, as was observed by Mr. Stewart, the most casual reader of Boethius cannot fail to be struck with the strong theism which breathes through his pages, and invites the touch of paraphrase to give it the full Christian sound, as when the city of Truth, from which Boethius represents himself as exiled, becomes under the translator's hand the heavenly Jerusalem ; a thought which is expressed in the recently discovered scholia. But in Lib. ii. metr. 4, where the translator brings in the striking sentence, " Christ dwelleth in the vale of Humility and at the monumental stone of Wisdom," the old Latin annotator contributes only this—" The stone is Christ." Of the famous simile which likens the world to an egg, there is this much found in the scholia—" That the sky and the earth and the sea are in configuration like an egg." See how this is developed by the poet :[1]—

Ðu gestaðoladest	Thou didst establish
þurh þa strongan meaht,	through strong might,
weroda wuldor cyning,	glorious king of hosts,
wunderlice	wonderfully
eorðan swa fæste	the earth so fast
þæt hio on ænige	that she on any
healfe ne heldeð,	side heeleth not,
ne mæg hio hider ne þider	nor can hither or thither
sigan þe swiðor	any more decline
þe hio symle dyde.	than she ever did.
Hwæt hi þeah eorðlices	Lo nothing earthly
auht ne haldeð,	at all sustains her,
is þeah efn eþe	it is equally easy
up and of dune	upwards and downwards
to feallanne	that there should be a fall
foldan þisse :	of this earth :
þæm anlicost	likest in fashion to
þe on æge bið	how in an egg

[1] The characters Þ þ and Ð ð are of identical value, meaning TH th.

gioleca on middan,	middlemost is the yolk,
glideð hwæþre	and withal gliding free
æg ymbutan .	the egg round about.
Swa stent eall weoruld	So standeth the world
stille on tille,	still in its place,
streamas ymbutan,	while streaming around,
lagufloda gelac,	water-floods play,
lyfte and tungla,	welkin and stars,
and sio scire scell	and the shining shell
scriðeð ymbutan	circleth about
dogora gehwilce ;	day by day now
dyde lange swa .	as it did long ago.

Book iii. metre 9 ; p. 182, ed. Sedgefield.

This simile occurs only in the poetical version of the Metres, for there are two versions, one in prose and another in verse, and it is agreed that the versification has been done after and from the prose ; but there is a question (into which we cannot now enter) whether Alfred is the author of both, or only of the prose version.

But before we quit Alfred's *Boethius*, we must notice his treatment of Lib. ii. prosa 7, where we may discover something more than free handling. In the first three lines of that section he found a profession of disinterestedness which he could honestly appropriate to himself. The Latin speaks thus : " Thou knowest, said I, that I was never governed by the ambition of transitory wealth. But material for action I did covet, that my talents might not rust in idleness." Upon these lines for a text the king made his chapter xvii., in which it is evident that he forgets Boethius and speaks for himself and of himself throughout. Applying his author's words to himself, he expands them into a veritable apology, explaining why a king needs a great revenue, and ending thus : "I resolved to live honourably as long as I lived, and after my time to leave to the men who should come after me my memorial in good works."

Now we come to the translation of the *Cura Pastoralis*, a work of high and manifold interest.[1] A copy of it was sent to every bishop in England. The very copy which was addressed to Werferth, Bishop of Worcester, is still in our possession. It is preserved in the Bodleian Library, and may be seen under glass by every visitor. This wonderful relic, like the Alfred Jewel, seems to bring us into personal contact with the great king himself.

In Alfred's Epistle to the bishops, which forms his Preface to the *Pastoralis*, the mind of the king is laid open in a very remarkable manner. Among the many precious evidences which time has spared for the perpetuation of a noble memory, the first place must certainly (on the whole) be accorded to this Preface. It exhibits in the clearest light the reflections of the king upon the past and present

---

[1] *King Alfred's West-Saxon Version of Gregory's Pastoral Care*, with an English translation, etc. By Henry Sweet, Esq., Balliol College, Oxford, 1871 and 1872. (Early English Text Society.)

condition of his country, his deep sense of the vast losses that had been sustained, his meditation on the means of repair at his command, and the direction of his thoughts to that which is the only root of effective reform, an enlightened and instructed national conscience. In his contemplation of this vital principle, he perceives the value of religious education, and the necessity of beginning there. At this point his discourse enters more into detail, the practical drift of which is, that the Latin schools being lost, and being (for the present at least) irreplaceable, it will be necessary to institute a system of education through the medium of the English language. Some scholars thought that education could only be properly conducted through Latin, and that the vernacular would lower its dignity and value. They could not wholly approve of the method of translations. Here Alfred had nearly the same battle to fight as Jerome fought before him, and in his apology he drew materials from Jerome's store, adding the further inference that if Scripture might be had in the vulgar tongue, why not other good books?

Children (he thought) should be taught to read English, and this elementary stage of education should be common to all of free birth. For the sons of those who could afford to prolong the education of their children, Latin studies should follow, and such boys should be trained for the higher offices.

Here the English basis of education is propounded as a course which was dictated by necessity; but if ever it should be demonstrated that this course is absolutely the best, the credit of having been the first to open the right path must not on that account be denied to King Alfred. In the good old times, Wessex had been far behind Northumbria in the culture of the classics, but this had led to a fuller development of the vernacular, and Alfred found his mother tongue not inadequate to the occasion, and large specimens of Latin literature were rendered in West Saxon, and thus it happened that the dialect of Wessex became to the after literature of England what the Attic dialect was to the literature of Greece.

The king's letter to the bishops begins thus:—

Ðeos bôc sceal to Wiogora Ceastre

This Book is to go to Worcester

Alfred, king, commandeth to greet Wærferth, bishop, with his words in loving and friendly wise: and I would have you informed that it has often come into my remembrance, what wise men there formerly were among the Angle race, both of the sacred orders and the secular; and how happy times those were throughout the Angle race; and how the kings who had the government of the folk in those days obeyed God and His messengers; and they on the one hand maintained their peace and their customs and their authority within their borders, while at the same time they spread their territory outwards; and how it then went well with them both in war and in wisdom ; and likewise the sacred orders, how earnest they were, as well about teaching as about learning, and about all the services that they owed to God ; and how people from abroad came to this land for wisdom and instruction ; and how we now should have to get them abroad if we were going to have them. So clean was it fallen away in the Angle race, that there were very few on this side Humber who would know how to render their services in English, or just read off an epistle out of Latin into English ; and I wean that not many would be on the other side Humber. So few of them were there that I cannot think of so much as a single one south of Thames when I took to the realm. God Almighty be thanked that we have now any teachers in office.

Moreover, the king called also to mind what he had himself seen in his early days, before all the harryings and burnings of recent times : how the churches of England had been well stored with books, and the clergy were numerous, but they had profited little by the books, because they could not understand them, as they were not written in their own language. At this point his eloquence rises to a dramatic pitch, and " It is," he breaks out, " as if they had said : ' Our ancestors, who were the masters of these sacred places, they loved wisdom, and by means of it they acquired wealth and left it to us. Here may yet be seen their traces, but we are not able to walk in their steps, forasmuch as we have now lost both the wealth and the wisdom, because we were not willing to bend our minds to that pursuit.'" Remembering all this, he had marvelled very exceedingly at those good scholars who were once so frequent in England, men who had completely mastered the Latin books, that they had not been willing to translate any part of them into their own language. But he soon answered himself and said, that they never could have anticipated the present utter decay, and it was their very zeal for learning which caused them to abstain from translating, because they thought that the path of education and knowledge lay through the study of languages.

Then I remembered how the law of Moses was first known in Hebrew; and later, when the Greeks had learned it, they translated it into their own language, and all other books too. And later still the Latin people in the same manner, they by means of wise interpreters, translated all the books into their own speech. And so also did all the other Christian nations translate some portion of the books into their own speech.

Therefore to me it seemeth better, if it seemeth so to you, that we also some books, those that most needful are for all men to be acquainted with, that we turn those into the speech which we all can understand, and that ye do as we very easily may with God's help, if we have the requisite peace, that all the youth which now is in England of free men, of those who have the means to be able to go in for it, be set to learning, while they are fit for no other business, until such time as they can thoroughly read English writing : afterwards further instruction may be given in the Latin language to such as are intended for a more advanced education, and are to be prepared for higher office. As I then reflected how the teaching of the Latin language had recently decayed throughout this people of the Angles, and yet many could read English writing, then began I among other various and manifold businesses of this kingdom to turn into English the book that is called *Pastoralis* in Latin, and *Hierdebóc* (Shepherding-Book) in English, sometimes word for word, sometimes sense for sense, just as I learned it of Plegmund my archbishop, and of Asser my bishop, and of Grimbald my priest, and of John my priest. After I had learned it so that I understood it and could render it with fullest meaning, I translated it into English ; and to each see in my kingdom I will send one ; and on each there is an " æstel " (ón ælcre bið án æstel), which is of the value of 50 mancuses. And I command in the name of God that no man remove the " æstel " from the book, nor the book from the minster. No one knows how long such learned bishops may be there, as now, thank God ! there are in several places ; and therefore I would that they (the books) should always be at the place ; unless the bishop should wish to have it with him, or it should be anywhere on loan, or any one should be writing another copy.

It has never been satisfactorily decided what kind of object is meant by the " æstel " which accompanied every one of the presentation copies of the *Hierdebóc*. Dr. Sweet translates thus : " And on each there is a clasp worth fifty mancus. And

I command in God's name that no man take the clasp from the book, or the book from the minster." Dr. Bosworth, in his Dictionary, explained æstel as a writing-tablet, and identified the word with "astula" in Du Cange. Now it is not easy to see the propriety of combining so personal a thing as a note-book with a volume designed for common use. Nor could such an object be a fixture upon the great book, which is what the king's phrase (ón ælcre bið) seems to require. On the other hand, Dr. Sweet's clasp is indeed a fixture, but of such a kind as to be a part of the book itself which could not be removed without wilful mutilation, and it does not appear that the king in his injunction is apprehensive of so flagrant an outrage as that.

My own impression is that the clue to the interpretation is furnished by a Glossary of the eleventh century, which gives "indicatorium" as the equivalent of æstel (Wright-Wülker, i. 327). I imagine a marker either of metal or of wood with metal fittings, so constructed as to be fixed upon the binding, and to bring a small plank across the page wherever desired. This would keep the parchment flat when apt to buckle, would mark the reader's or transcriber's place, and would minimise the risk of injury by fingering. It would be attached to one of the boards only in a movable way, perhaps with a screw, and consequently would require a strict and imperative rule to secure it from misplacement. The derivation might well be from "astula" (= assula).

This great epistolary Preface is followed by a second, of another theme and another type. The first is conceived in the statesmanlike spirit of a king who is meditating of civil order and education in a country that has almost lapsed into barbarism. The second is the utterance of the literary artist concerning the book he has translated, the author and his merits, and the weight of his authority, not disregarding the history and transmission of the very codex over which he has been at work. The first of these prefaces is in strong and ragged prose; the second is in heroic verse, which recalls the tradition that Alfred was fond of the old songs of his native land.

<pre>
    Þis ærendgewrit   Agustinus
    ofer sealtne sæ   suðan brohte
    ieg-buendum,   swa hit ær fore
    adihtode   drihtnes cempa
  5 Rome papa.   Ryhtspell monig
    Gregorius gleawmod   gind wód
    ðurh sefan snythro   searoðonca hord.
    Forðæm he monncynnes mæst gestriende
    rodra wearde,   Romwara betest,
 10 monna módwelegost,   mærðum gefrægost.

    Siððan min on Englisc   Ælfred kyning
    awende worda gehwelc,   and me his writerum
    sende suð and norð ;   heht him swelcra má
</pre>

    brengan bi ðære bisene,   ðæt he his biscepum
15 sendan meahte   forðæm hi his sume ðorften,
    ða ðe Lædenspræce   læste cuðon.

I append an alliterative translation, which runs almost line for line :—

    This epistle   Augustine
    over salt sea   brought from the south
    to us island-dwellers,   just as it erst
    indited had been   by Christ's doughty soldier
  5. the Roman pontiff.   Much right discourse
    did Gregory of glowing wit   give forth apace
    with skilful soul,   a hoard of studious thought.
    He of mankind   converted the most
    to the Ruler of heaven :   he of Romans the best,
10. of men the most learned   and widest admired.

    At length into English,   Alfred the King
    wended[1] my every word: and me to his writers
    south and north sent out ;   more copies of such
    he bade them bring back,   that he to his bishops
15. might send,   for some of them needed it,
    those who with Latin speech   had least acquaintance.

A few notes may be useful here. In the first line the expression " This epistle " applies to the entire work, because it is addressed by Gregory to John, Bishop of Ravenna, and opens with a dedication in epistolary form.

The poet has a warm feeling for the very

---

[1] My excuse for using an obsolete word is that it is Alfred's own, and I could not do without it. Moreover, I was fortified by the hope that some poet might adopt it and revive its transitival use.

manuscript he has been bending over, which he venerates as a sacred relic, because it was one of the books which were brought to this island by Augustine, Gregory's chosen missionary.

In lines 8-10 is there not a reminiscence of the closing lines of the *Beowulf?*

At verse 11 there is an abrupt transition, and the after part is in an altered manner. The book itself becomes the speaker, and in the diction we recognise the manner of him who dictated to his goldsmith the now famous legend :

ÆLFRED MEC HEHT GEWYRCAN.

In line 12 we should particularly note the assertion which is couched in the words " awende worda gehwelc," a marked and idiomatic phrase which may be represented in Latin thus : " vertit verborum quodque," *i.e.* translated every word. This does not point to any rule or restriction in the manner of rendering, as if the translator had tasked himself to a verbal fidelity, for in his first preface, speaking of this very work, he had plainly said that he had sometimes rendered word by word and sometimes sense for sense (hwilum word be worde, hwilum andgit of andgite). But what he meant to say was this, that whereas in his other translations he had used his originals as passive material to be wrought upon and converted as his own design and purpose guided him, he had treated Gregory's

Pastoral Care as he would treat Scripture, wherein nothing could be added nor taken away.

To conclude the subject of Alfred's Gregory's *Pastoral Care*, let it be noted, that not only is it one of the books which are said to have been translated by the king, but the statement is made by himself speaking in the first person, and with a singular circumstantiality, and that besides this the book is distinguished by three peculiar incidents : (1) That the translation was entire ; (2) that a copy of it was sent to every bishop ; (3) that the king was pleased to celebrate the memorable history of the copy upon which he had worked.

As the chief of Alfred's translations the *Hierdebóc* has naturally taken up much of our space, and we must now be brief on the *Dialogues*. And indeed we have the less to say because the Alfredian version has not yet been edited.[1] It exists in three manuscripts of the eleventh century, one in the Cotton Library, and the other two at Oxford and Cambridge. This translation is reputed to have been made by Werferth, Bishop of Worcester, but the authority for this statement is late and of doubtful value. There is no mention of it in the preface, where the king speaks in the first person, and acknowledges the services of friends who had acted as transcribers. It runs thus :—

---

[1] It is said that a critical edition, based upon the three manuscripts, is in preparation by Herr Hans Hecht.

"I, Alfred, by the grace of Christ, dignified with the honour of royalty, have assuredly understood, and through the reading of holy books have often heard, that we to whom God hath given so much eminence of worldly distinction, have peculiar need at times to humble and subdue our minds to the divine and spiritual law, in the midst of this earthly anxiety; and I accordingly sought and requested of my trusty friends that they for me, out of pious books about the conversation and miracles of holy men, would transcribe the instruction that hereinafter followeth : that I, through the admonition and love being strengthened in my mind, may now and then contemplate the heavenly things in the midst of these earthly troubles."

Such is the preface in the two manuscripts at Oxford and Cambridge ; but in lieu of this the Cotton manuscript has a preface in high-pitched archaic and stilted prose wherein the book speaks and sets forth that it was transcribed by order of a Bishop Wulfstan from a copy that was given him by King Alfred, whose name is glorified with romantic superlatives of eulogy. This is poor apocryphal stuff, but yet as a glimpse at the posthumous cultus of Alfred's fame it is interesting and even valuable.[1]

Bede's *History* was the most modern of the books on Alfred's list. In this book the translator

[1] This bizarre composition was published by Dr. Krebs in *Anglia*, iii. (1880).

omitted considerable sections and added none.
There is no contemporary record that the translator was King Alfred. The earliest extant statement of the kind is in Ælfric's *Homily on St.
Gregory's Day*, where the preacher, referring to
" Historia Anglorum," as he calls it, adds, " which
King Alfred translated out of Latin into English."
Though a hundred years later, this is nevertheless
excellent testimony, and it has been supported
both by later historians and until recently by
modern critics.

But now the latest editor,[1] Mr. Thomas Miller,
has pointed out some radical differences of dialect
between the West Saxon of the *Cura Pastoralis*
and the English of this translation, which he
locates in the northern part of Mercia. He is
further guided by certain ecclesiastical considerations (especially the contents of the parts omitted)
to select Litchfield as the spot where the translation
was probably made. The evidence is too multi-
farious to be stated here, but it seems worthy to
receive a searching examination and discussion.

So far we have treated of the more conspicuous
and better-known of the king's writings ; we must
now make mention of his minor works. In
" The Shrine : a Collection of Occasional Papers
on Dry Subjects," which appeared at irregular

---

[1] Yet there is a later edition proceeding from the press, by Dr. Schipper,
Professor of English at Vienna.

intervals from 1864 to 1870, the Rev. Oswald Cockayne published for the first time two works which claim to rank among Alfredian literature. These he entitled, *King Ælfred's Book of Martyrs* and *Blooms by King Ælfred*.

The *Blooms* are a translation or adaptation of Augustine's Soliloquies and his Epistle to Paulina on the Vision of God, intermingled with extracts from the *City of God* and from Gregory, and from Jerome, and withal many passages that appear to be original. The English of the book is a debased Saxon of the twelfth century. The title *Blooms* is a translation of " blostman," which is repeatedly used of the work in the Anglo-Saxon text. There is a preface, in which the work is spoken of under another figure—that of collecting material to build a house. At the close we read, " Here end the sayings which King Alfred collected." Lappenberg classed the book (then unprinted) among the apocryphal works of the king, and Pauli thought that some compiler of the twelfth century had used the name of the king whose memory was still dear to the people. But in 1877 Professor Wülker took it up, and he soon changed the aspect of the case. He showed, in a highly convincing manner, that this book has an intimate relation with Alfred's *Boethius*, that it carries on an argument which was broached there, and that the two books must be from the same hand. His inference is that it was done after the *Boethius*, and that it was (apparently) the latest work upon which the king was engaged. In 1894 the affinity between the two books was further confirmed by Mr. Frank G. Hubbard in *Modern Language Notes*. Specially convincing are two brief touches in chapter xvii., which echo the argument of the similarly numbered chapter in Alfred's *Boethius* which I have called an apology. The book is in an imperfect state.

The *Book of Martyrs* is also imperfect, beginning at December 31 with St. Columba, and ending with St. Thomas, December 21. The first day of January is called "the eighth Yule day" (se eahteða geohhel dæg). There are four manuscripts of this book, and one of them, a fragment of two leaves, appears to be of Alfred's time. Moreover, of the saints which are recorded none are later than the ninth century. Another argument is that under November 15 is given a Life of St. Milus, which must (says Cockayne) have been brought direct from Syria to England, and probably from Helias, the patriarch of Jerusalem, with whom Alfred had a correspondence, according to the nearly contemporary *Leech Book*. These evidences appear to Wülker to justify the conclusion of Cockayne, "that the Martyr Book here presented was at least in use in Ælfred's time, and was probably then composed."

We must now mention some titles of books imputed to the king. By the third generation after Alfred the tradition of his literary activity had already assumed mythical proportions. The Latin historian Æthelweard says that nobody knows how many volumes he produced (*volumina numero ignoto*). William of Malmesbury says that at the time of his death he was working at a translation of the Psalter. There is a poetical work of maxims and proverbs in which each of the detached sentences begins with "Thus said Alfred." This book opens with an assembly of notables at Seaford, presided over by King Alfred, the Shepherd and Darling of England. These Proverbs of Alfred appear to be a composition of the twelfth century. Moreover, he is said to have translated into English the Fables of Æsop. He is also credited with a treatise on Falconry.

But if in one direction the tradition has reached a fabulous extreme, it is possible, on the other hand, that there may still remain something of his which has been overlooked or has not been adequately recognised. I allude to the Saxon Chronicle, about the king's relation to which there is doubtless more to be said than has yet found a place in literature. To speak but of one section— I never can read the annals of 893-897 without seeming to hear the voice of King Alfred. Among the illuminations of the approaching anniversary, we may hope that a clearer light will be shed upon this interesting question.

The Will of Alfred is a very remarkable document, and opens to us more than might be expected of family arrangements as to property. That coupling of the names of Æþered and Ælfred which has such a singular and conspicuous appearance in the Chronicle receives some very practical illustration. There were at that time no professional men to make Wills, and we have no cause to doubt that the diction is Alfred's, as it purports to be, being indited in the first person. There is much in this document to provoke inquiry and research, and it would probably repay the diligent student for a closer investigation than it has hitherto received.

In our time when books are freely produced in great abundance, it is hard to appreciate the power and originality of King Alfred's work in the field of literature. When we look about for his motives we find such as these : need of occasional retirement and solace in the midst of harassing affairs, desire for personal improvement and edification, strong intellectual appetites, etc.—but all these controlled by one chief and dominant purpose, that of national education. Looking at the external aspect of the king's situation we might have judged it sufficient for him at that time to concentrate his energies upon the restoration of material prosperity and the strengthening of the national armaments.

That the prior necessity of these was not over-looked, we have ample proof in the subsequent progress of Wessex. But this did not satisfy the kingly ambition of Alfred; he craved for his people the higher benefits of political life, their moral and intellectual and spiritual development. Curiosity may well prick us to ask from what source far-reaching aims like these so suddenly burst into our history, and that, too, at a time of exhaustion at home and apprehension from abroad. If King Alfred saw a connection between general education and the acquisition of wealth (as there is some indication that he did), this may partly explain the energy of his educational policy, but we still desiderate something more. If we might assume that being under a strong sense of what he had himself gained by his early education, he desired to impart the like advantages to his people, then and only then the problem would find its appropriate and adequate solution.

The beginnings of modern education in the seventh century were quickened with the sense that something had been lost, and the whole movement was coloured with the sentiment of retrieval and recovery. Two great historical exhibitions of this effort are displayed in the Latin schools of Anglia and of Charlemagne, which are in fact but two parts of one movement, linked together by the name of Alcuin.

King Alfred's educational revival is isolated from the preceding by the wars and desolations of the Wicingas, and it starts with a new basis in the installation of the mother tongue as the medium of elementary teaching. To this innovation it is due that we alone of all European nations have a fine vernacular literature in the ninth and tenth and eleventh centuries. And the domestic culture of that era, I take it, was the cause why the great French immigration which followed in the wake of the Norman Conquest did not finally swamp the English language.

ENGLISH LAW BEFORE THE
NORMAN CONQUEST

By Sir Frederick Pollock

ENGLISH LAW BEFORE THE NORMAN CONQUEST [1]

AT first sight Anglo-Saxon law may appear merely barbarous to the modern reader. In order to be just to it we must consider its surroundings.

Anglo-Saxon life was rough and crude as compared not only with any modern standard but with the amount of civilisation which survived, or had been recovered, on the Continent. There was very little foreign trade, not much internal traffic, nothing like industrial business of any kind on a large scale, and (it need hardly be said) no system of credit. Such conditions gave no room for refined legal science applied by elaborate legal machinery, such as those of the Roman Empire had been and those of modern England and the commonwealths that have sprung from her were

---

[1] A chapter from a work in preparation, reprinted here, with some omissions and alterations, from the *Law Quarterly Review*.

to be.   Such as the men were, such had to be the rules and methods whereby some kind of order was kept among them.   Our ancestors before the Norman Conquest lived under a judicial system, if system it can be called, as rudimentary in substance as it was cumbrous in form.   They sought justice, as a rule, at their primary local court, the court of the hundred, which met once a month, and for greater matters at a higher and more general court, the county court, which met only twice a year, except, perhaps, for merely formal business.   We say purposely met rather than sat.   The courts were open-air meetings of the freemen who were bound to attend them, the *suitors* as they are called in the terms of Anglo-Norman and later medieval law ; there was no class of professional lawyers ; there were no judges in our sense of learned persons specially appointed to preside, expound the law, and cause justice to be done; the only learning available was that of the bishops, abbots, and other great ecclesiastics.   This learning, indeed, was all the more available and influential because, before the Norman Conquest, there were no separate ecclesiastical courts in England.   There were no clerks nor, apparently, any permanent officials of the popular courts ; their judgments proceeded from the meeting itself, not from its presiding officer, and were regularly preserved only in the memory of the suitors.   A modern student or man of business will at first sight wonder how this rude and scanty provision for judicial affairs can have sufficed even in the Dark Ages. But when we have reflected on the actual state of Anglo-Saxon society, we may be apt to think that at times the hundred and the county court found too little to do rather than too much. The materials for what we now call civil business practically did not exist.

There is now no doubt among scholars that the primary court was the hundred court. If the township had any regular meeting (which is quite uncertain), that meeting was not a judicial body. The King, on the other hand, assisted by his Council of wise men, the Witan,[1] had a superior authority in reserve. It was allowable to seek justice at the king's hands if one had failed, after due diligence, to obtain it in the hundred or the county court. Moreover the Witan assumed jurisdiction in the first instance where land granted by the king was in question, and perhaps in other cases where religious foundations or the king's great men were concerned. Several examples of such proceedings are recorded, recited as we should say in modern technical speech, in extant land-charters which declare and confirm the result of

---

[1] There is more authority for this short form than for the fuller Witena-Gemót (not witenágemot as sometimes mispronounced by persons ignorant of Old-English inflexions).

disputes, and therefore we know more of them than we do of the ordinary proceedings in the county and hundred courts, of which no written record was kept. But they can have had very little bearing, if any, on the daily lives of the smaller folk. In important cases, the county court might be strengthened by adding the chief men of other counties ; and, when thus reinforced, there is hardly anything to distinguish it from the Witan save that the king is not there in person.[1] The king might act as arbitrator or give advice to his immediate dependents to compromise their suits ; but there was no regular way of appealing from the judgments of the popular courts.

Some considerable time before the Norman Conquest, but how long is not known, bishops and other great men had acquired the right of holding courts of their own and taking the profits in the shape of fines and fees, or what would have been the king's share of the profits. My own belief is that this began very early, but there is no actual proof of it. Twenty years after the Conquest, at any rate, we find private jurisdiction constantly mentioned in the Domesday Survey, and common in every part of England : about the same time, or very shortly afterwards, it was re-

---

[1] Such a court, after the Conquest, was that which restored and confirmed the rights of the see of Canterbury on Penenden Heath : but it was held under a very special writ from the king.

cognised as a main ingredient in the complex and artificial system of feudalism. After having grown in England, as elsewhere, to the point of threatening the king's supremacy, but having happily found in Edward I. a master such as it did not find elsewhere before the time of Richelieu, the manorial court is still with us in a form attenuated almost to the point of extinction. It is not material for the later history of English law to settle exactly how far the process of concession or encroachment had gone in the time of Edward the Confessor, or how fast its rate was increasing at the date of the Conquest. There can be no doubt that on the one hand it had gained and was gaining speed before "the day when King Edward was alive and dead," [1] or on the other hand that it was further accelerated and emphasised under rulers who were familiar with a more advanced stage of feudalism on the Continent. But this very familiarity helped to make them wise in time ; and there was at least some foreshadowing of royal supremacy in existing English institutions. Although the courts of the hundred and the county were not the king's courts, the king was bound by his office to exercise some general supervision over their working. He was represented in the county court by the sheriff ; he might send out commissioners to inquire and report how justice was done, though he could not inter-

---

[1] The common form of reference in Domesday Book.

fere with the actual decisions. The efficiency of these powers varied in fact according to the king's means and capacity for exercising them. Under a wise and strong ruler like Alfred or Æthelstan they might count for much; under a feeble one like Æthelred they could count for very little.

A modern reader fresh to the subject might perhaps expect to find that the procedure of the old popular courts was loose and informal. In fact it was governed by traditional rules of the most formal and unbending kind. Little as we know of the details, we know enough to be sure of this; and it agrees with all the evidences we have of the early history of legal proceedings elsewhere. The forms become not less but more stringent as we pursue them to a higher antiquity; they seem to have not more but less appreciable relation to any rational attempt to ascertain the truth in disputed matters of fact. That task, indeed, appears to have been regarded as too hard or too dangerous to be attempted by unassisted human faculties. All the accustomed modes of proof involved some kind of appeal to supernatural sanctions. The simplest was the oath of one of the parties, not by way of testimony to particular facts, but by way of assertion of his whole claim or defence; and this was fortified by the oaths of a greater or less number of helpers, according to the nature of the case and the importance of the persons concerned, who swore with him that his oath was true. He lost his cause without a chance of recovery if any slip was made in pronouncing the proper forms, or if a sufficient number of helpers were not present and ready to make the oath. On the other hand the oath, like all archaic forms of proof, was conclusive when once duly carried through. Hence it was almost always an advantage to be called upon to make the oath of proof, and this usually belonged to the defendant. "Gainsaying is ever stronger than affirming . . . Owning is nearer to him who has the thing than to him who claims."[1] Our modern phrase "burden of proof" is quite inapplicable to the course of justice in Anglo-Saxon courts : the benefit or " prerogative " of proof, as it is called even in modern Scottish books, was eagerly contended for. The swearer and his oath-helpers might perjure themselves, but if they did there was no remedy for the loser in this world, unless he was prepared to charge the court itself with giving false judgment. Obviously there was no room in such a scheme for what we now call rules of evidence. Rules there were, but they declared what number of oath-helpers was required, or how many common men's oaths would balance a thegn's. In the absence of manifest facts, such as a fresh wound, which could be shown to the court, an oath called

---

[1] *Æthelr.* ii. 9.

the " fore-oath " was required of the complainant in the first instance as a security against frivolous suits.   This was quite different from the final oath of proof.

Oath being the normal mode of proof in disputes about property, we find it supplemented by ordeal in criminal accusations.   A man of good repute could usually clear himself by oath ; but circumstances of grave suspicion in the particular case, or previous bad character, would drive the defendant to stand his trial by ordeal.   In the usual forms of which we read in England the tests were sinking or floating in cold water,[1] and recovery within a limited time from the effects of plunging the arm into boiling water or handling red-hot iron.   The hot-water ordeal at any rate was in use from an early time, though the extant forms of ritual, after the Church had assumed the direction of the proceedings, are comparatively late.   Originally, no doubt, the appeal was to the god of water or fire, as the case might be.   The Church objected, temporised, hallowed the obstinate heathen customs by the addition of Christian ceremonies, and finally, but not until the thirteenth century, was strong enough to banish them.   As a man was not put to the ordeal unless he was disqualified

---

[1] There is a curious French variant of the cold-water ordeal in which not the accused person, but some bystander taken at random, is immersed : I do not know of any English example.

from clearing himself by oath for one of the reasons above mentioned, the results were probably less remote from rough justice than we should expect, and it seems that the proportion of acquittals was also larger. Certainly people generally believed to be guilty did often escape, how far accidentally or otherwise we can only conjecture.[1] Another form of ordeal favoured in many Germanic tribes from early times, notwithstanding protest from the Church, and in use for deciding every kind of dispute, was trial by battle : but this makes its first appearance in England and Scotland not as a Saxon but as a distinctly Norman institution.[2] It is hard to say why, but the fact is so. It seems from Anglo-Norman evidence that a party to a dispute which we should now call purely civil sometimes offered to prove his case not only by oath or combat, but by ordeal, as the court might award. This again suggests various explanations of which none is certain.[3]

Inasmuch as all the early modes of proof involved large elements of unknown risk, it was

---

[1] The cold-water ordeal was apparently most feared ; see the case of Ailward, *Materials for Hist. St. Thomas*, i. 156, ii. 172 ; Bigelow, *Plac. A.-N.* 260. For a full account, see Lea, *Superstition and Force.*

[2] See more in Neilson, *Trial by Combat*, an excellent and most interesting monograph.

[3] Cases from D. B. collected in Bigelow, *Plac. A.-N.* 40-44, 61. Even under Henry II. we find, in terms, such an offer, but it looks, in the light of the context, more like a rhetorical asseveration—in fact the modern " j'en mettrais ma main au feu "—than anything else : *op. cit.* 196.

rather common for the parties to compromise at the last moment. Also, since there were no ready means of enforcing the performance of a judgment on unwilling parties, great men supported by numerous followers could often defy the court, and this naturally made it undesirable to carry matters to extremity which, if both parties were strong, might mean private war. Most early forms of jurisdiction, indeed, of which we have any knowledge, seem better fitted to put pressure on the litigants to agree than to produce an effective judgment of compulsory force. Assuredly this was the case with those which we find in England even after the consolidation of the kingdom under the Danish dynasty.

Rigid and cumbrous as Anglo-Saxon justice was in the things it did provide for, it was, to modern eyes, strangely defective in its lack of executive power. Among the most important functions of courts as we know them is compelling the attendance of parties and enforcing the fulfilment both of final judgments and of interlocutory orders dealing with the conduct of proceedings and the like. Such things are done as of course under the ordinary authority of the court, and with means constantly at its disposal; open resistance to judicial orders is so plainly useless that it is seldom attempted, and obstinate preference of penalties to submission, a thing which now and then happens, is counted a mark of eccentricity bordering on unsoundness of mind. Exceptional difficulties, when they occur, indicate an abnormal state of the commonwealth or some of its members. But this reign of law did not come by nature; it has been slowly and laboriously won. Jurisdiction began, it seems, with being merely voluntary, derived not from the authority of the State but from the consent of the parties. People might come to the court for a decision if they agreed to do so. They were bound in honour to accept the result; they might forfeit pledges deposited with the court, or put their neighbours who had become sureties in an awkward position; but the court could not compel their obedience any more than a tribunal of arbitration appointed at this day under a treaty between sovereign States can compel the rulers of those States to fulfil its award. Anglo-Saxon courts had got beyond this most early stage, but not very far beyond it.

The only way to bring an unwilling adversary before the court was to take something of his as security till he would attend to the demand; and practically the only things that could be taken without personal violence were cattle. Distress in this form was practised and also regulated from a very early time. It was forbidden to distrain until right had been formally demanded—in Cnut's time to the extent of three summonings—and refused.

Thus leave of the court was required, but the party had to act for himself as best he could. If distress failed to make the defendant appear, the only resource left was to deny the law's protection to the stiff-necked man who would not come to be judged by law. He might be outlawed, and this must have been enough to coerce most men who had anything to lose and were not strong enough to live in rebellion ; but still no right could be done to the complainant without his submission. The device of a judgment by default, which is familiar enough to us, was unknown, and probably would not have been understood. An elaborate system of never trusting one man without two or more sureties (to describe it roughly) was used to supplement these defects, and we may suppose it to have been more or less effective, though clumsy and tedious.

Final judgment, when obtained, could in like manner not be directly enforced. The successful party had to see to gathering the " fruits of judgment," as we say, for himself. In case of continued refusal to do right according to the sentence of the court, he might take the law into his own hands, in fact wage war on his obstinate opponent. The ealdorman's aid, and ultimately the king's, could be invoked in such extreme cases as that of a wealthy man, or one backed by a powerful family, setting the law at open defiance.

But this was an extraordinary measure, analogous to nothing in the regular modern process of law.

The details of Anglo-Saxon procedure and judicial usage had become or were fast becoming obsolete in the thirteenth century, which is as much as to say that they were already outworn when the definite growth of the Common Law began. But the general features of the earlier practice, and still more the ideas that underlay them, have to be borne in mind. They left their stamp on the course of our legal history in manifold ways; many things in the medieval law cannot be understood without reference to them; and even in modern law their traces are often to be found.

While the customary forms of judgment and justice were such as we have said, there was a comparatively large amount of legislation or at least express declaration of law ; and, what is even more remarkable, it was delivered in the mother tongue of the people from the first. Æthelberht, the converted king of Kent, was anxious to emulate the civilisation of Rome in secular things also, and reduced the customs of his kingdom, so far as might be, to writing ; but they were called *dooms*, not *leges ;* they were issued in English, and were translated into Latin only after the lapse of some centuries. Other Kentish princes, and afterwards Ine of Wessex, followed the example ; but the regular series of Anglo-Saxon laws begins towards the end of the ninth century with Alfred's publication of his own dooms, and (it seems) an amended version of Ine's, in which these are now preserved. Through the century and a half between Alfred's time and Cnut's [1] legislation was pretty continuous, and it was always in English. The later restoration of English to the statute roll after the medieval reign of Latin and French was not the new thing it seemed. It may be that the activity of the Wessex princes in legislation was connected with the conquest of the Western parts of England, and the need of having fixed rules for the conduct of affairs in the newly settled districts. No one doubts that a considerable West-Welsh population remained in this region, and it would have been difficult to apply any local West-Saxon custom to them.

Like all written laws, the Anglo-Saxon dooms have to be interpreted in the light of their circumstances. Unluckily for modern students, the matters of habit and custom which they naturally take for granted are those of which we now have least direct evidence. A large part of them is filled by minute catalogues of the fines and com-

---

[1] The so-called laws of Edward the Confessor, an antiquarian compilation of the twelfth century largely mixed with invention, do not even profess to be actual dooms of the Confessor, but the customs of his time collected by order of William the Conqueror.

positions payable for manslaughter, wounding, and other acts of violence.   We may well suppose that in matters of sums and number such provisions often express an authoritative compromise between the varying though not widely dissimilar usages of local courts ; at all events we have an undoubted example of a like process in the fixing of standard measures after the Conquest ; and in some of the later Anglo-Saxon laws we get a comparative standard of Danish and English reckoning. Otherwise we cannot certainly tell how much is declaration of existing custom, or what we should now call consolidation, and how much was new.   We know from Alfred's preamble to his laws, evidently framed with special care, that he did innovate to some extent, but, like a true father of English statesmen, was anxious to innovate cautiously. On the whole the Anglo-Saxon written laws, though of priceless use to students of the times, need a good deal of circumspection and careful comparison of other authorities for using them aright.   It is altogether misleading to speak of them as codes, or as if they were intended to be a complete exposition of the customary law.

We pass on to the substance of Anglo-Saxon law, so far as capable of being dealt with in a summary view.   There were sharp distinctions between different conditions of persons, noble, free, and slave.   We may talk of "serfs" if we like, but the Anglo-Saxon "theow" was much more like a Roman slave than a medieval villein. Not only slaves could be bought and sold, but there was so much regular slave-trading that selling men beyond seas had to be specially forbidden. Slaves were more harshly punished than free men, and must have been largely at their owner's mercy, though there is reason to think that usage had a more advanced standard of humanity than was afforded by any positive rules. Manumission was not uncommon, and was specially favoured by the Church. The slave had opportunities (perhaps first secured under Alfred) for acquiring means of his own, and sometimes bought his freedom.

Among free men there were two kinds of difference. A man might be a lord having dependents, protecting them and in turn supported by them, and answerable in some measure for their conduct ; or he might be a free man of small estate dependent on a lord. In the tenth century, if not before, every man who was not a lord himself was bound to have a lord on pain of being treated as unworthy of a free man's rights ; "lordless man" was to Anglo-Saxon ears much the same as "rogue and vagabond" to ours. This wide-spread relation of lord and man was one of the elements that in due time went to make up feudalism. It was not necessarily associated with any holding of land by the man from the lord, but the association was doubtless already common a long time before the Conquest, and there is every reason to think that the legally uniform class of dependent free men included many varieties of wealth and prosperity. Many were probably no worse off than substantial farmers, and many not much better than slaves.

The other legal difference between free men was their estimation for *wergild*, the " man's price " which a man's kinsfolk were entitled to demand from his slayer, and which sometimes he might have to pay for his own offences; and this was the more important because the weight of a man's oath also varied with it. A *thegn* (which would be more closely represented by " gentilhomme " than by " nobleman ") had a wergild six times as great as a *ceorl's*[1] or common man's, and his oath counted for six common oaths before the court.[2] All free men, noble or simple, looked to their kindred as their natural helpers and avengers ; and one chief office of early criminal law was to regulate the blood-feud until there was a power strong enough to supersede it.

We collect from the general tenor of the Anglo-

---

[1] The modern forms of these words, *thane* and *churl*, have passed through so much change of meaning and application that they cannot be safely used for historical purposes.

[2] There were minor distinctions between ranks of free men which are now obscure, and were probably no less obscure in the thirteenth century : they seem to have been disregarded very soon after the Conquest.

Saxon laws that the evils most frequently calling for remedy were manslaying, wounding, and cattle-stealing ; it is obvious enough that the latter, when followed by pursuit in hot blood, was a natural and prolific source of the two former. The rules dealing with such wrongs or crimes (for archaic laws draw no firm line between public offence and private injury) present a strange contrast of crude ideas and minute specification, as it appears at first sight. Both are however really due to similar conditions. A society which is incapable of refined conceptions, but is advanced enough to require equal rules of some kind and to limit the ordinary power of its rulers, is likewise incapable of leaving any play for judicial discretion. Anglo-Saxon courts had not the means of apportioning punishment to guilt in the particular case, or assessing compensation according to the actual damage, any more than of deciding on the merits of conflicting claims according to the evidence. Thus the only way remaining open was to fix an equivalent in money or in kind for each particular injury : so much for life and so much for every limb and member of the human body. The same thing occurs with even greater profusion of detail in the other Germanic compilations of the Dark Ages. In the latter days of Anglo-Saxon monarchy treason was added to the rude catalogue of crimes, under continental influence ultimately derived from Roman law ; but the sin of plotting against the sovereign was the more readily conceived as heinous above all others by reason of the ancient Germanic principle of faith between a lord and his men. This prominence of the personal relation explains why down to quite modern times the murder of a husband by his wife, of a master by his servant, and of an ecclesiastical superior by a clerk, secular or regular, owing him obedience, were specially classed as " petit treason" and distinguished from murder in general.[1]

Secret murder as opposed to open slaying was treated with special severity. This throws no light on our later criminal law ; nor has it much to do with love of a fair fight, though this may have strengthened the feeling ; rather it goes back to a time when witchcraft, and poisoning as presumably connected therewith, were believed to. be unavoidable by ordinary caution, and regarded with a supernatural horror which is still easy to observe among barbarous people. With these exceptions, and a few later ones of offences reserved for the king's jurisdiction, crimes were not classified or distinguished in Anglo-Saxon custom save by the amount of public fine[2] and private composition

---

[1] Blackstone, *Com.* iv. 203.

[2] *Wite* was probably, in its origin, rather a fee to the court for arranging the composition than a punishment. But it is treated as penal from the earliest period of written laws. In the tenth century it could mean pain or torment ; see C. D. 1222 *ad fin.*

required to redeem the wrong-doer's life in each case. Capital punishment and money payment, or rather liability to the blood-feud redeemable by money payment, and slavery for a thief who could not make the proper fine, were the only means of compulsion generally applicable, though false accusers and some other infamous persons were liable to corporal penalties. Imprisonment is not heard of as a substantive punishment; and it is needless to say that nothing like a system of penal discipline was known. We cannot doubt that a large number of offences, even notorious ones, went unpunished. The more skilled and subtle attacks on property, such as forgery and allied kinds of fraud, did not occur, not because men were more honest, but because fraudulent documents could not be invented or employed in a society which knew nothing of credit and did not use writing for any common business of life.

Far more significant for the future development of English law are the beginnings of the King's Peace. In later times this became a synonym for public order maintained by the king's general authority; nowadays we do not easily conceive how the peace which lawful men ought to keep can be any other than the Queen's or the commonwealth's. But the king's justice, as we have seen, was at first not ordinary but exceptional, and his power was called to aid only when other means had failed.   To be in the king's peace was to have a special protection, a local or personal privilege. Every free man was entitled to peace in his own house, the sanctity of the homestead being one of the most ancient and general principles of Teutonic law.   The worth set on a man's peace, like that of his life, varied with his rank, and thus the king's peace was higher than any other man's. Fighting in the king's house was a capital offence from an early time.   Gradually the privileges of the king's house were extended to the precincts of his court, to the army, to the regular meetings of the shire and hundred, and to the great roads. Also the king might grant special personal protection to his officers and followers ; and these two kinds of privilege spread until they coalesced and covered the whole ground.   The more serious public offences were appropriated to the king's jurisdiction ; the king's peace was used as a special sanction for the settlement of blood-feuds, and was proclaimed on various solemn occasions ; it seems to have been specially prominent—may we say as a " frontier regulation "?—where English conquest and settlement were recent.[1]   In the generation before the Conquest it was, to all appearance, extending fast.   In this kind of development the first stage is a really exceptional right ; the second is a right which has to be distinctly claimed, but is open

---

[1] See the customs of Chester, D. B. i. 262 b, extracted in Stubbs, *Sel. Ch.*

to all who will claim it in the proper form ; the third is the " common right " which the courts will take for granted.   The Normans found the king's peace nearing, if not touching, the second stage.

Except for a few peculiar provisions, there is nothing in Anglo-Saxon customs resembling our modern distinctions between wilful, negligent, and purely accidental injuries.   Private vengeance does not stop to discriminate in such matters, and customary law which started from making terms with the avenger could not afford to take a more judicial view.   This old harshness of the Germanic rules has left its traces in the Common Law down to quite recent times.   A special provision in Alfred's laws recommends a man carrying a spear on his shoulder to keep the point level with the butt ; if another runs on the point so carried, only simple compensation at most [1] will be payable.   If the point has been borne higher (so that it would naturally come in a man's face), this carelessness may put the party to his oath to avoid a fine.   If a dog worried or killed any one, the owner was answerable in a scale of fines rising after the first offence ; [2] the indulgence of the modern law which requires knowledge of the dog's habits was unknown.   But it may be doubted whether these

---

[1] Ælf. 36.   The statement is rather obscure.   One is tempted to suppose that an accident of that kind had happened to some well-known person at the king's court.

[2] Ælf. 23.

rules applied to anything short of serious injury. Alfred's wise men show their practical sense by an explanatory caution which they add : the owner may not set up as an excuse that the dog forthwith ran away and was lost. This might otherwise have seemed an excellent defence according to the archaic notion that the animal or instrument which does damage carries the liability about with it, and the owner may free himself by abandoning it (*noxa caput sequitur*).[1]

We have spoken of money payments for convenience ; but it does not seem likely that enough money was available, as a rule, to pay the more substantial wergilds and fines ; and it must once have been the common practice for the pacified avenger to accept cattle, arms, or valuable ornaments, at a price agreed between the parties or settled by the court. The alternative of delivering cattle is expressly mentioned in some of the earlier laws.

As for the law of property, it was rudimentary, and inextricably mixed up with precautions against theft and charges of theft. A prudent buyer of cattle had to secure himself against the possible claim of some former owner who might allege that the beasts had been stolen. The only way to do this was to take every step in public and with good witness. If he set out on a journey to a fair, he

---

[1] See Holmes, *The Common Law*, 7-12.

would let his neighbours know it. When he did business either far or near, he would buy only in open market and before credible persons, and, if the sale were at any distance from home, still more if he had done some trade on the way without having set out for the purpose, he would call the good men of his own township to witness when he came back driving his newly-gotten oxen, and not till then would he turn them out on the common pasture. These observances, probably approved by long-standing custom, are prescribed in a whole series of ordinances on pain of stringent forfeitures.[1] Even then a purchaser whose title was challenged had to produce his seller, or, if he could not do that, clear himself by oath. The seller might produce in turn the man from whom he had bought, and he again might do the like; but this process ("vouching to warranty" in the language of later medieval law) could not be carried more than three steps back, to the "fourth hand" including the buyer himself. All this has nothing to do with the proof of the contract in case of a dispute between the original parties to the sale; it is much more aimed at collusion between them, in fact at arrangements for the receipt and disposal of stolen goods. The witnesses to the sale are there not for the parties' sake, but as a check in the public interest. We are tempted at first sight to think

---

[1] See especially Edg. iv. 6-11.

of various modern enactments that require signature or other formalities as a condition of particular kinds of contracts being enforceable ; but their provisions belong to a wholly different category.

Another archaic source of anxiety is that borrowed arms may be used in a fatal fight and bring the lender into trouble. The early notion would be that a weapon used for manslaying should bring home the liability with it to the owner, quite regardless of any fault ; which would afterwards become a more or less rational presumption that he lent it for no good purpose. Then the risk of such weapons being forfeited continued even to modern times. Hence the armourer who takes a sword or spear to be repaired, and even a smith who takes charge of tools, must warrant their return free from blood-guiltiness, unless it has been agreed to the contrary.[1] We also find, with regard to the forfeiture of things which " move to death," that even in case of pure accident, such as a tree falling on a woodman, the kindred still have their rights. They may take away the tree if they will come for it within thirty days.[2]

There was not any law of contract at all, as we now understand it. The two principal kinds of transaction requiring the exchange or acceptance of promises to be performed in the future were marriage and the payment of wergild. Apart from

---

[1] Ælf. 19.   [2] Ælf. 13.

the general sanctions of the Church, and the king's special authority where his peace had been declared, the only ways of adding any definite security to a promise were oath and giving of pledges. One or both of these were doubtless regularly used on solemn occasions like the settlement of a blood-feud ; and we may guess that the oath, which at all events carried a spiritual sanction, was freely resorted to for various purposes. But business had hardly got beyond delivery against ready money between parties both present, and there was not much room for such confidence as that on which, for example, the existence of modern banking rests. How far the popular law took any notice of petty trading disputes, such as there were, we are not informed ; it seems likely that for the most part they were left to be settled by special customs of traders, and possibly by special local tribunals in towns and markets. Merchants trafficking be-yond seas, in any case, must have relied on the customs of their trade and order rather than the cumbrous formal justice of the time.

Anglo-Saxon landholding has been much dis-cussed, but is still imperfectly understood, and our knowledge of it, so far from throwing any light on the later law, depends largely on what can be inferred from Anglo-Norman sources. It is certain that there were a considerable number of independent free men holding land of various amounts down to the time of the Conquest.   In the eastern counties some such holdings, undoubtedly free, were very small indeed.[1]   But many of the lesser free men were in practical subjection to a lord who was entitled to receive dues and services from them ; he got a share of their labour in tilling his land, rents in money and kind, and so forth.   In short they were already in much the same position as those who were called villeins in the twelfth and thirteenth centuries.   Also some poor free men seem to have hired themselves out to work for others from an early time.[2]   We know next to nothing of the rules under which free men, whether of greater or lesser substance, held " folk-land," that is, estates governed by the old customary law.   Probably there was not much buying and selling of such land.   There is no reason to suppose that alienation was easier than in other archaic societies, and some local customs found surviving long after the Conquest point to the conclusion that often the consent of the village as well as of the family was a necessary condition of a sale.   Indeed it is not certain that folk-land, generally speaking, could be sold at all.   There is equally no reason to think that ordinary free landholders could dispose of their land by will, or were in the habit of making wills for any purpose.

---

[1] Maitland, *Domesday Book and Beyond*, 106.
[2] Ælf. 43.

Anglo-Saxon wills (or rather documents more like a modern will than a modern deed) exist, but they are the wills of great folk, such as were accustomed to witness the king's charters, had their own wills witnessed or confirmed by bishops and kings, and held charters of their own ; and it is by no means clear that the lands dealt with in these wills were held as ordinary folk-land. In some cases it looks as if a special licence or consent had been required ; we also hear of persistent attempts by the heirs to dispute even gifts to great churches.[1]

Soon after the conversion of the south of England to Christianity, English kings began to grant the lordship and revenues of lands, often of extensive districts, to the Church, or more accurately speaking to churches, by written charters framed in imitation of continental models. Land held under these grants by charter or "book," which in course of time acquired set forms and characters peculiar to England, was called *bookland*, and the king's bounty in this kind was in course of time extended to his lay magnates. The same extraordinary power of the king, exercised with the witness and advice[2] of his Witan, which could confer a title to princely revenues, could also confer

---

[1] See C. D. 226 compared with 256.

[2] A strictly accurate statement in few words is hardly possible. See the section " Book-land and Folk-land " in Maitland, *Domesday Book and Beyond*, p. 244 *sqq.*

large disposing capacities unknown to the customary
law ; thus the fortunate holder of bookland might
be and often was entitled not only to make a grant
in his lifetime or to let it on such terms as he
chose, but also to leave it by will.   My own
belief is that the land given by the Anglo-Saxon
wills which are preserved was almost always book-
land even when it is not so described.   Indeed
these wills are rather in the nature of postponed
grants, as in Scotland a "trust disposition" had
to be till quite lately, than of a true last will and
testament as we now understand it.   They certainly
had nothing to do with the Roman testament.

Long before the Conquest it had become the
ambition of every man of substance to hold book-
land, and we may well think that this was on the
way to become the normal form of land-ownership.
But this process, whatever its results might have
been, was broken off by the advent of Norman
lords and Norman clerks with their own different
set of ideas and forms.

The various customs of inheritance that are to
be found even to this day in English copyholds,
and to a limited extent in freehold land, and which
are certainly of great antiquity, bear sufficient
witness that at least as much variety was to be
found before the Conquest. Probably the least
usual of the typical customs was primogeniture ;
preference of the youngest son, ultimogeniture or

junior-right as recent authors have called it, the " borough-English " of our post-Norman books, was common in some parts ; preference of the youngest daughter, in default of sons, or even of the youngest among collateral heirs, was not un-known.　But the prevailing type was equal division among sons, not among children including daughters on an equal footing as modern systems have it.　Here again the effect of the Norman Conquest was to arrest or divert the native lines of growth.　In this country we now live under laws of succession derived in part from the military needs of Western Europe in the early Middle Ages, and in part from the cosmopolitan legislation of Justinian, the line between the application of the two systems being drawn in a manner which is accounted for by the peculiar history of our institutions and the relations between different jurisdictions in England, but cannot be explained on any rational principle.　But the unlimited freedom of disposal by will which we enjoy under our modern law has reduced the anomalies of our intestate succession to a matter of only occasional inconvenience.

Small indeed, it is easy to perceive, is the portion of Anglo-Saxon customs which can be said to have survived in a recognisable form.　This fact nevertheless remains compatible with a perfectly real and living continuity of spirit in our legal institutions.

If we do not nowadays observe King Alfred's dooms, or anything like them, still we owe it to the work of Alfred and his children that England was saved to become an individual nation, and that our fundamental ideas of justice have survived all external changes. Those ideas may be summed up very shortly. Justice is essentially public ; the business of parties is to conduct their cases according to the rules of law, the business of the court is to hear and determine between them, not to conduct an inquiry ; judicial interpretation of the law is the only authentic and binding interpretation, and in particular the executive has no such power. These principles appear obvious to most of us, but there are many civilised countries where they are not admitted. We can trace them back to the rudest beginnings of our jurisprudence ; they are as vigorous as ever, in all the complexity of modern affairs, wherever the English tongue is spoken.

ALFRED AND THE ARTS

By Rev. W. J. Loftie

ALFRED AND THE ARTS

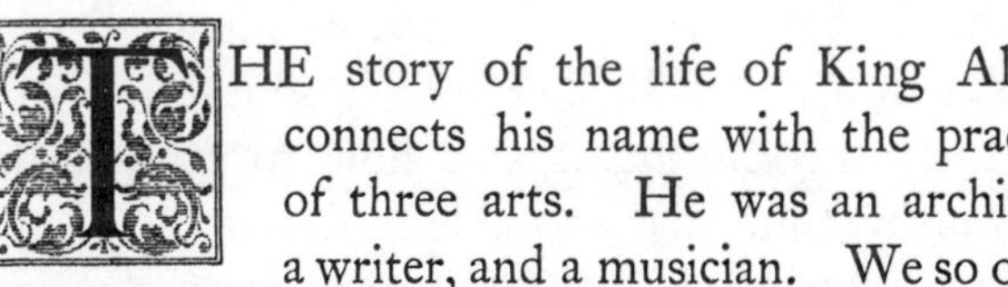HE story of the life of King Alfred connects his name with the practice of three arts. He was an architect, a writer, and a musician. We so often hear of the art of war that when we remember his proficiency as a soldier we are inclined to forget that fortification, fighting, fishing, and hunting, if they may be called arts, are not fine arts. Alfred's noble defence of England against the Danes has ever since his day been an example to his countrymen of later generations. He first taught them the negative virtue that consists in not knowing when they are beaten. But our concern, in the particular chapter that has fallen to my lot, is with Alfred and the fine arts : and as you cannot enjoy painting or music without a house, it behoves us to inquire first as to the state of architecture in the ninth century, and as to the part taken by Alfred in building houses, churches, and cities. We must remember that though, as we know, writing and the illumination of manuscripts had

attained a very high pitch of excellence, Alfred had no maps to guide him. His workmen may have been able to scratch their diagrams on stones, and in other similar ways to obtain guidance in carrying out such buildings as the king required. But he had traversed all that part of England over which he reigned, and was as well acquainted with the marshes of Somerset as with the wooded valley of the Lea and the chalk cliffs of his southern shore. He knew how to build and how to handle the ships of his time, and was able to defeat the Danes on what might be called their own element. Tradition has always and plausibly assigned to him a further feat of naval warfare. When his enemies had sailed up to Hertford and prepared to rest for the winter and mend their boats, he, so to speak, drew the water from under them by the knowledge which prompted him to divide the channels. The object of this and other achievements of the kind was his anxiety to obtain the command of the great estuary into which the Fleet, the Wallbrook, the Lea, and the creeks about Barking fell. To gain this region was one thing, to hold it another. The Saxons before his time disliked the use of walls in warfare. Still more they disliked the trouble of building and maintaining them. But Alfred possessed whatever was known of fortification, and by this knowledge he was able to raise the first permanent impediment in the way of future invaders.

The best authorities agree that to Alfred rather than to the Romans must be ascribed the foundation of London as it was during the Middle Ages, and as, in a sense, it is still. Stow, as far back as the reign of Queen Elizabeth, citing some long-lost document or tradition, tells us that Alfred found London empty. He, to use a very modern expression, " restored " the walls. He rebuilt them with the material at hand, namely, the material with which another Saxon king had built the church of St. Alban. The Saxons had disdained to fight behind walls in their conquest of the degenerate and Romanised Britons. But the Danes were as fighting men equal to the Saxons. Some advantage was needed before the Saxons could overcome their formidable invaders. He saw two important points to be gained by the restoration of London : first, that his new city would be virtually impregnable by the Danes ; secondly, that the situation would be that from which he could best defend the whole valley of the Thames. As the Thames rises in Gloucestershire, and runs thence to Essex and Kent, this was to defend all his English dominions. We say now that to hold the Nile is to hold all Egypt and much more. In those days, when the river was the chief highway, to protect the Thames was to protect Kent, Wessex, and Mercia. I have mentioned hunting as an art. Alfred had an eye for a hunting country, as we say now. London was seen by him as we see Pevensey, a ruined wall enclosing nothing. There may have been vestiges of a church. There may have been the piers of a bridge. There can have been little else. Alfred made the bridge into a fortress, renewing the great timbers which had connected the piers. The bridge stood a long way farther down the stream than the modern London Bridge, and to defend it the king built a tower at the south-east corner of the restored wall. William the Conqueror, like Alfred, saw the advantages of the site, and here he placed the tower which still stands, a relic of his reign, a reminiscence of that of his great predecessor. The Roman roads through the city, and the gates by which they made their exit, no longer existed, or, at best, were ruined and useless. He made one road diagonally from the bridge across his market-place to Westgate, which we know as Newgate. A second road led to what we still call Bishopsgate, some distance westward from the site of a Roman gate which opened on the old roads to Lincoln and into Essex. His corn-market, where there was a weighing-stone for wheat, stood to the west of the Market Place or Cheap. A road along the northern side of the Cheap was in existence so soon after Alfred's time that it must have been planned if it was not made by him. We call it Cheapside, and here there are traditions of a king's palace near the spot where, centuries later, the great men of the city began to assemble in their Guildhall.

We have mentioned Alfred's wall. His outline, we may be sure, was speedily filled up. St. Paul's Church rose among the wooden and brick houses. Civic institutions began to show themselves where there was security; and Alfred's brother-in-law, Burgred, the last King of Mercia, had a house in Coleman Street, and gave the cabbage garden to the Bishop of Worcester. Alfred's daughter, Æthelflæd, married Æthelred, Burgred's successor, who was called the Alderman of the Mercians. To him, and after his death to his widow, the king committed the charge and governance of the city, and Æthelbert became the first alderman of London. The importance of the place is apparent. It was the easternmost bulwark of Alfred's kingdom against the settled Danes of East Anglia, as well as against the fresh incursions of pirates and filibusters from over the sea. Alfred's prescience is proved by one single fact. From that day to this London has never been taken by force of arms. The Danes from the North Sea never got past the Tower—the Danes from the Danelaw never broke through the wall.

With regard to ecclesiastical architecture in Alfred's time we know very little; with regard to civil architecture scarcely anything. The church

of St. Lawrence, Bradford-on-Avon, is assigned
by competent judges to as late a date as the ninth
century ; but Aldhelm, who was Bishop of Sherborn
near the beginning of the seventh century, founded
a nunnery at Bradford, which was afterwards
connected with that of Shaftesbury, and the
church is mentioned as early as the time of King
Æthelred, just a hundred years after the death of
Alfred. Building-stone of the best kind abounds
in the neighbourhood, as well as in that of Deerhurst, near Tewkesbury. The stone masonry
suggests that wooden buildings set the pattern in
both places : while, from the ease with which St.
Paul's in London was burnt, both before and after
the Norman Conquest, we may be sure it contained
very little brickwork. Deerhurst was built in
1053, so we must not look to it as an example of
the architecture of Alfred's time. At Wing, near
Aylesbury, the chancel is Saxon, and not unlike St.
Lawrence's chapel in its peculiar flat panelling. It
is very lofty, but less narrow in proportion than
Bradford, and has a series of very interesting vaulted
crypts, in which we see a good many thin bricks of
the kind usually ascribed to the Romans, fragments
perhaps of a Roman fortress or a villa at that
place. Several towers with early Saxon features
remain, but many have lately been destroyed, as at
St. Albans, Limpsfield, and other places. A few
fragments of Beda's time may possibly remain

THE SEASONS—OCTOBER TO DECEMBER

in the very ancient church of Jarrow. Saxon building with Roman bricks is to be seen at St. Martin's, Canterbury, and at Dover, but both falsified by injudicious alterations. Where good building-stone comes to the surface, as in Northamptonshire, we find not far apart examples of churches and towers which may well have existed at the beginning of the tenth century. Barnack and Earls Barton may be named, and with them should be classed St. Michael's at Oxford, and St. Benedict's at Cambridge. Traces of Saxon work are often found in old churches, but they can seldom be dated in the age of Alfred. It may, in fact, be laid down as a rule that where there were no fortifications, building was of but a temporary character, and where stone did not greatly abound, churches were made of wood and were very perishable. In a few places towers were built specially, like the Irish round towers, for storage and defence. In these cases we usually find great height in proportion, and an arrangement of the entrance so that it can only be reached by a ladder, such as we may still trace in the Tower of London, the keep of which had no entrance on the ground level before the reign of Henry VIII. Of dwelling-houses we see no examples. In London, as much as two centuries later, ordinances were made for the improvement of town dwellings, but that previously this branch of architecture had been sadly neglected we may infer from reading that even chimneys were usually made of wood.

We know that castles were built by Alfred, and in his time, but in a majority of cases they consisted only of mounds and stockades, strengthened by great beams and balks of timber. To withstand attacks like those of the Danes, sudden and usually brief, these defences may have been very powerful. At a few places like Tamworth, where some supposed Saxon masonry is still pointed out, or at Colchester, where, as at London, Roman walls were restored, a little building took the place of woodwork. Mr. Clark, the best authority about *Medieval Military Architecture*, says plainly that though " the English were from a remote period conversant with masonry, and constructed churches of stone or timber as suited them best," they avoided everything but timber where they made a mound or an artificial earthwork of any kind. The Norsemen from the mouth of the Elbe were not very different from the Danes and the Saxons, Jutes and Angles were only earlier immigrants from the same regions. It is not possible now to distinguish the earthworks thrown up by Alfred and his men from those of the Danes which they overthrew. One thing only we can recognise as his peculiar work, namely, the formation in his own mind of clearly devised plans by which, with inferior strength, with fewer men and arms, and in face of frequent disaster, he was able to consolidate his power, to turn even defeat into success, and at last, before his early death, both to obtain a time of respite for his people and to show them how in the future they might always hopefully resist the invader. If the Danish attack was for the moment overwhelming, it was desultory. The defence offered by Alfred was far-seeing, part of a consistent whole, a scheme which must eventually prevail.

In 876 the pirates attacked Wareham successfully, and thence fell upon Exeter : but in 878 Alfred made his famous camp in the Somerset marshes, and by slow degrees drove them northward and eastward, established himself in London, and fortified it, thence expelling them from Gravesend, from Rochester, from Farnham, from their great timber fort at Benfleet, until Hasting, the Danish leader, in 893, submitted to Alfred and was converted and baptized. Finally, in 897 the war was over. The Danes had thrown up a work "on the Lea, twenty miles from London, whereupon Ælfred," says Mr. Clark, "threw up another work on each bank of that river lower down, and diverted the waters through a number of shallow courses, thus effectually shutting in the Danish ships." From this time to the end of his life, a brief period of about four years, Alfred devoted himself to the arts of peace. Among them he reckoned ship-building and the codification of the laws, but we chiefly remember his love of books, his establishment of schools, in which writing was practised as a fine art, and his encouragement of skilful work in gold, enamel, and inlay.

Many examples remain to show us that art of this last kind, as well as poetry and music, were largely and successfully practised among the Anglo-Saxons. The great discoveries in grave mounds in Kent, of which the results may be seen in the Mayer Museum at Liverpool, prove that from a very early period there were among the people skilful designers and artificers, not only in jewellery, but in glass. The well-known ornament preserved at Oxford, probably a royal badge, which bears his name, is perhaps the most familiar object which can be connected with him. We may remember of Alfred, as well as of King Edwin of Northumbria and of other law-loving monarchs, that he hung up gold bracelets by the wayside, and that none dared to steal them. Unfortunately for another story connecting Alfred with the fine arts, it is not older than the twelfth century. The fact that such a legend existed shows us what was the popular estimate of the king's character. We are glad therefore to observe that Freeman finds nothing impossible in the story that " Alfred, wishing to know what the Danes were about and how strong they were, set out one day from Athelney in the disguise of a minstrel or juggler, and went into the Danish camp and stayed there several days, amusing the Danes with his playing, till he had seen all that he wanted, and then went back without any one finding him out." Alfred's dealings with the Danes, whether in disguise or otherwise, led to the defeat and conversion of Guthorm, to the peace of Wedmore, and to two incidents in which pictorial art has a place : the capture of the Raven standard, and the cutting of one of the figures of a horse on the side of the chalk downs. There are two such white horses, one near Edington, which has been " restored," the other near Shrivenham, "which has not been altered at all, but is very old and rude, so that you might hardly know that it was meant for a horse at all."

The pretty story of Alfred's youth, as to his learning to read, will not, unfortunately, bear critical examination. That it should have been so long believed and so often told is, however, eloquent as to the reputation he acquired as a boy. Some have even doubted if he could read, but in his journey to Rome he learned Latin—at least it is more probable that he knew Latin than that he was ignorant of it. He was certainly desirous, during his scanty leisure from warfare, to further the cause of learning by all means in his power. His monks at Athelney and his nuns at Shaftesbury were expressly devoted to the labours of the scriptorium, and when we observe the number of the books which, in spite of the Danes, were produced in England in the course of the eighth and ninth centuries, we are forced to the conclusion that the powers of the time were unanimously in favour of the art of writing. We may, indeed, go much further than this. After a careful comparison, such as may be made in the British Museum, or any other great public library, we are forced to the conclusion that no country in Europe at that time could boast of the production of such beautiful books, filled with such skilful writing and illustrated with such exquisite pictures, as England in the reign of King Alfred. A well-known manuscript (Addl. MSS. 34, 890) produced by the monks of Alfred's own monastery at Winchester, or the volume of Gospels and other readings written without illustrations at Canterbury, cannot be surpassed in all the qualities which we admire in manuscripts. Italy itself could do nothing even approaching the *Psychomachia* of Prudentius, probably written at Shaftesbury in the ninth century. It is filled with figures representing the soul in conflict with evil. They are wrongly described as "tinted," but the figures and their draperies are drawn in two colours, in outline, in a manner which would not surprise us on a Greek vase of the best period. We admire in a relief by Donatello, or a fresco by Giotto, similar art, centuries later. Of the same period, or earlier, is a book reciting the names of the benefactors of Lindisfarne—St. Cuthbert was Alfred's special patron—in which the lettering is partly in black, partly in gold, worthy of a *Liber Vitæ*. In many volumes we see such an initial as that which figures in the story mentioned above, among them copies of Beowulf's or Cædmon's poems, such as might very well answer to the book of old songs which Alfred's mother was said to have shown him. (Cottonian MSS. Vit. A. xv.)

The famous *Benedictional* written for Æthelwold, Bishop of Winchester, some fifty years after Alfred's time, may be taken to show us to what perfection this art was brought. The style is that to which the artists of his time were tending. Here and there, among older books, we may trace features which occur in this sumptuous volume, both among the figure-subjects and among the ornaments. Sir Digby Wyatt, an excellent judge, is enthusiastic on the manuscript, yet fails to appreciate the figure-subjects, because they show "little classical influence." I am not inclined to find fault on that account. The opinion of a learned antiquary of the last generation, John Gage, should have great weight. He looked upon the *Benedictional* as the culmination of the art of the Anglo-Saxon school; and John Young Ottley expressed himself in equally eulogistic terms about the manuscript, which is in the collection of the Duke of Devonshire and which was fully described and in great part engraved by the Society of Antiquaries in 1832 (*Archæologia*, vol. xxiv.) Ottley points out its chief claim on our admiration thus : " You desire from me a few words on the illuminations in St. Æthelwold's Benedictionary, with my opinion of their merits as works of art. I feel honoured by the request, and comply with it the more willingly as I can honestly say that I think them in the highest degree creditable to the taste and intelligence of this nation at a period when in most parts of Europe the fine arts are commonly believed to have been at a very low ebb." Farther on, Ottley speaks of " the justness of the general proportions of the figures." He especially praises some little angels holding scrolls, which, he says, " have so much gracefulness and animation, are so beautifully draped, and so well adapted in their attitudes to the spaces they occupy, that I hardly know how to praise them sufficiently."

The mechanical part of the work should be carefully examined. It shows—and not it alone, but many early books as well—that in the time of Alfred artists could command the help of artificers who knew how to make vellum fit for the most delicate painting and writing ; that colours were produced worthy of the vellum for which they were prepared ; that gold-beating and gilding with the leaf had been carried to a perfection never since surpassed.   Godeman, the monk, afterwards, in 970, abbot of Thorney, who wrote the book, must have been born during the reign of Alfred, or soon after, and learned his art from the writers of the great king who, in his English translation of the Pastoral of Gregory, remarks feelingly on the destruction wrought by the Danes, and how before their incursions " the churches throughout Britain were filled with treasures and books."

INDEX